The Z Notation
A Reference Manual

Prentice Hall International
Series in Computer Science

C. A. R. Hoare, Series Editor

BACKHOUSE, R. C., *Program Construction and Verification*
BACKHOUSE, R. C., *Syntax of Programming Languages: Theory and practice*
DEBAKKER, J. W., *Mathematical Theory of Program Correctness*
BIRD, R., and WADLER, P., *Introduction to Functional Programming*
BJÖRNER, D., and JONES, C. B., *Formal Specification and Software Development*
BORNAT, R., *Programming from First Principles*
BUSTARD, D., ELDER, J., and WELSH, J., *Concurrent Program Structures*
CLARK, K. L., and MCCABE, F. G., *micro-Prolog: Programming in logic*
CROOKES, D., *Introduction to Programming in Prolog*
DROMEY, R. G., *How to Solve it by Computer*
DUNCAN, F., *Microprocessor Programming and Software Development*
ELDER, J., *Construction of Data Processing Software*
GOLDSCHLAGER, L., and LISTER, A., *Computer Science: A modern introduction (Now in 2nd edn)*
GORDON, M. J. C., *Programming Language Theory and its Implementation*
HAYES, I. (ed.), *Specification Case Studies*
HEHNER, E. C. R., *The Logic of Programming*
HENDERSON, P., *Functional Programming: Application and implementation*
HOARE, C. A. R., *Communicating Sequential Processes*
HOARE, C.A.R., and SHEPHERDSON, J. C. (eds), *Mathematical Logic and Programming Languages*
HUGHES, J. G., *Database Technology: A software engineering approach*
INMOS LTD, *occam Programming Manual*
INMOS LTD, *occam 2 Reference Manual*
JACKSON, M. A., *System Development*
JOHNSTON, H., *Learning to Program*
JONES, C. B., *Software Development: A Rigorous Approach (OOP)*
JONES, C. B., *Systematic Software Development using VDM*
JONES, G., *Programming in occam*
JONES, G., and GOLDSMITH, M., *Programming in occam 2*
JOSEPH, M., PRASAD, V. R., and NATARAJAN, N., *A Multiprocessor Operating System*
LEW, A., *Computer Science: A mathematical introduction*
MACCALLUM, I., *Pascal for the Apple*
MACCALLUM, I., *UCSD Pascal for the IBM PC*
MARTIN, J. J., *Data Types and Data Structures*
MEYER, B., *Object-oriented Software Construction*
PEYTON JONES, S. L., *The Implementation of Functional Programming Languages*
POMBERGER, G., *Software Engineering and Modula-2*
REYNOLDS, J. C., *The Craft of Programming*
RYDEHEARD, D. E., and BURSTALL, R. M., *Computational Category Theory*
SLOMAN, M., and KRAMER, J., *Distributed Systems and Computer Networks*
SPIVEY, J. M., *The Z Notation: A Reference Manual*
TENNENT, R. D., *Principles of Programming Languages*
WATT, D. A., WICHMANN, B. A., and FINDLAY, W., *ADA: Language and methodology*
WELSH, J., and ELDER, J., *Introduction to Modula-2*
WELSH, J., and ELDER, J., *Introduction to Pascal (Now in 3rd edn)*
WELSH, J., ELDER, J., and BUSTARD, D., *Sequential Program Structures*
WELSH, J., and HAY, A., *A Model Implementation of Standard Pascal*
WELSH, J., and MCKEAG, M., *Structured System Programming*
WIKSTRÖM, Å., *Functional Programming using Standard ML*

The Z Notation
A Reference Manual

J.M. Spivey

Programming Research Group
Oxford University Computing Laboratory

Based on the work of

J. R. Abrial, I. J. Hayes, C. A. R. Hoare,
He Jifeng, C. C. Morgan, J. W. Sanders,
I. H. Sørenson, J. M. Spivey, B. A. Sufrin

Prentice Hall
New York   London   Toronto   Sydney   Tokyo

First published 1989 by
Prentice Hall International (UK) Ltd,
66 Wood Lane End, Hemel Hempstead,
Hertfordshire, HP2 4RG
A division of
Simon & Schuster International Group

Printed and bound in Great Britain by
BPCC Wheatons Ltd, Exeter

Library of Congress Cataloging-in-Publication Data

Spivey, J. M.
    The Z notation.
    (Prentice-Hall International series in computer
science)
    "November 1987."
    Bibliography: p.
    Includes index.
    1. Z (Computer program language) I. Title.
II. series.
QA76.73.Z2S66   1987   005.13'3   88-23174
ISBN 0-13-983768-X

British Library Cataloguing in Publication Data

Spivey, J. M.
    The Z notation : a reference manual.
    (Technical monography PRG).—(Prentice Hall
International series in computer science).
    1. Computer systems. Programming languages :
    Z language
    I. Title   II. Series
    005.13'3
    ISBN 0-13-983768-X

---

2 3 4 5   92 91 90 89

Contents

Preface

JACK: You're quite perfect, Miss Fairfax.
GWENDOLEN: Oh! I hope I am not that. It would leave no room for developments, and I intend to develop in many directions.

Oscar Wilde, *The Importance of Being Earnest*

The Z notation for specifying and designing software has evolved over the best part of a decade, and it is now possible to identify a standard set of notations which, although simple, capture the essential features of the method. This is the aim of the reference manual in front of you, and it is written with the everyday needs of readers and writers of Z specifications in mind. It is not a tutorial, for a concise statement of general rules is often given rather than a presentation of illustrative examples; nor is it a formal definition of the notation, for an informal but rigorous style of presentation will be more accessible to Z users, who may not be familiar with the special techniques of formal language definition.

It is perhaps worth recording here the causes which led to even this modest step towards standardization of Z. The first of these is the growing trend towards computer assistance in the writing and manipulation of Z specifications. While the specifier's tools amounted to little more than word-processing facilities, they had enough inherent flexibility to make small differences in notation unimportant. But tools are now being built which depend on syntactic analysis, and to some extent on semantic analysis, of specifications. For these tools – syntax checkers, structure editors, type checkers, and so on – to be useful and reliable, there must be agreement on the grammatical rules of the language they support.

Communication between people is also helped by an agreed common notation, and here I expect the part of this manual devoted to the standard 'mathematical tool-kit' to be especially useful. In this part, I have given a formal definition of each mathematical symbol, together with an informal description and a collection of useful algebraic laws relating the symbol to others.

A third reason for standardization is the need to define a syllabus for training courses in the use of Z. Whilst there is an important difference between learning the Z language and learning to be effective in reading and writing Z specifications, just as learning to program is much more than learning a programming language, I hope that this description of the language will provide a useful check-list of topics to be covered in courses.

Finally, as the use of Z increases, there will be a need for a reference point for contracts and research proposals which call for a specification to be written in Z, and this manual is intended to fill this need also.

In selecting the language features and the mathematical symbols to be included, I have tried to maintain a balance between comprehensiveness and simplicity. On one hand, there is a need to promote common notations for as many important concepts as possible; but on the other hand, there is little point in including notations which are used so rarely that they will be forgotten before they are needed. This observation principally affects the choice of symbols to be included in the 'mathematical tool-kit'.

Because one of the aims is increased stability of Z, I have felt obliged to omit from the account certain aspects of Z which still appear to be tentative. I found it difficult to reconcile the idea of *overloading* – that is, the possibility that two distinct variables in the same scope might have identical names – with the idea that common components are identified when schemas are joined, so overloading is forbidden in the language described. The relative weakness of the Z type system would, in any case, make overloading less useful than it is in other languages.

More importantly, I have also felt unable to include a system of formal inference rules for deriving theorems about specifications. The principles on which such a system might be based are clear enough, at least for the parts of Z which mirror ordinary mathematical notation; but the practical usefulness of inference rules seems to depend crucially on making them interact smoothly, and we have not yet gained enough experience to do this.

How to use this book

Here is a brief summary of the contents of each chapter:

Chapter 1 is an overview of the Z notation and its use in specifying and developing programs. The chapter begins with a simple example of a Z specification; this is followed by examples of the use of the schema calculus to modularize a specification and the use of data refinement to relate specifications and designs.

Chapter 2 explains the concepts behind the Z language, such as *schemas* and *types*. It contains definitions of the terms which are used later to explain the constructs of Z. Although the presentation is informal, it assumes a basic knowledge of naive set theory and predicate calculus.

Chapter 3 contains a description of the Z language itself. It is organized according to the syntactic categories of the language, with separate sections on declarations, predicates, expressions, and so on. Some more advanced features of the language, *generics* and *free types*, are given their own sections at the end of the chapter.

Chapter 4 describes a standard collection of mathematical symbols which are useful in specifying information systems. It is divided into six sections, each dealing with a small mathematical theory such as sets, relations or sequences. The chapter starts with a classified list of the symbols it defines, on pages 86 to 88.

Chapter 5 explains the conventions used in describing sequential programs with Z specifications, including the processes of operation and data refinement, by which abstract specifications can be developed into more concrete designs.

Chapter 6 contains a summary of the syntax of Z. It is here that the fine details of Z syntax are presented, such as the relative binding powers of operators, connectives and quantifiers.

Large parts of Chapters 3 and 4 are organized into 'manual pages' with a fixed layout. Each manual page deals with a single construct or symbol, or a small group of related ones. In Chapter 3, the pages may contain the following items:

Name The constructs defined on the page are listed, and a short descriptive title is given for each of them.

Syntax The syntax rules for each construct are given in BNF.

Scope rules If variables are introduced by a construct, this item identifies the region of text in the specification where they are visible. If the meaning of a construct depends implicitly on the values of certain variables, these variables are listed.

Type rules The type of each kind of expression is described in terms of the types of its sub-expressions. Restrictions on the types of sub-expressions are stated.

Description The meaning of each construct is explained informally.

Laws Some mathematical properties of the constructs and relationships with other constructs are listed.

In Chapter 4, the format is a little different: each mathematical symbol is defined formally in an item headed '**Definition**', using the Z notation itself. Particular emphasis is laid on the collection of mathematical laws obeyed by the symbols. For brevity, the variables used in these laws are not declared explicitly if their types are clear from the context. An item headed '**Notation**' sometimes explains special-purpose notations designed to make the symbols easier to use.

Several special pages in Chapter 4 consist entirely of laws of a certain kind: for example, the laws which express the monotonicity with respect to $\subseteq$ of various operations on sets and relations are collected on page 103 under the title 'Monotonic operations'.

As well as the usual entries under descriptive terms, the general index at the back of the book contains entries for each syntactic class of the language such as Expression or Paragraph. These entries appear in sans-serif type, and refer to the syntax rules for the class. Each symbol defined as part of the mathematical tool kit has an entry, either under the symbol itself, if it is a word such as *head*, or under a descriptive name if it is a special symbol such as $\oplus$. These special symbols also appear in the one-page 'Index of special symbols'.

The glossary at the back of the book contains concise definitions of the technical terms used in describing Z. Each term defined in the glossary is set in *italic* type the first time it appears in the text.

Acknowledgements

It is my pleasure to end this preface by thanking my present and former colleagues for allowing me to contribute to the work of theirs reported in this book; many of the ideas are theirs, and I am pleased that their names appear with mine on the title-page. I owe a special debt of thanks to Bernard Sufrin, whose *Z Handbook* was the starting-point for this manual, and whose constant advice and encouragement have helped me greatly. I should like to thank all those who have pointed out errors and suggested possible improvements, and especially the following, who have helped me with detailed comments on the manuscript: Tim Clement (University of Manchester), Anthony Hall (Praxis Systems), Nigel Haigh (Seer Management), Ian Hayes (University of Queensland), Steve King (University of Oxford), Ruaridh MacDonald (Royal Signals and Radar Establishment), Sebastian Masso (University of Oxford), Dan Simpson (Brighton Polytechnic), Sam Valentine (Logica).

I am grateful to Katharine Whitehorn for permission to quote from her book *Cooking in a Bedsitter*. Chapter 1 is adapted from a paper which first appeared in *Software Engineering Journal* under the title 'An introduction to Z and formal specifications', and is reproduced with the permission of the Institute of Electrical Engineers.

My final thanks go to my wife Petronella, who contributed large helpings of the two most vital ingredients, patience and food, even when I seemed to spend more time with the TEXbook than I did with her.

Oriel College, Oxford   J. M. S.
September, 1988

You probably cannot afford elaborate equipment, and you certainly have no room for it: but the *right* simple tools will stop you longing for the other, complicated ones.

Katharine Whitehorn, *Cooking in a Bedsitter*

CHAPTER ONE

Tutorial Introduction

This chapter is an introduction to some of the features of the Z notation, and to its use in specifying information systems and developing
rigorously-checked designs. The first part introduces the idea of a formal specification using a simple example: that of a 'birthday book',
in which people's birthdays can be recorded, and which is able to
issue reminders on the appropriate day. The behaviour of this system for correct input is specified first, then the schema-calculus is
used to strengthen the specification into one requiring error reports
for incorrect input.

The second part of the chapter introduces the idea of data refinement as a means of constructing designs which achieve a formal specification. Refinement is presented through the medium of two examples;
the first is a direct implementation of the birthday book from part one,
and the second is a simple checkpoint facility, which allows the current
state of a database to be saved and later restored. A Pascal-like programming language is used to show the code for some of the operations
in the examples.

1.1 What is a formal specification?

Formal specifications use mathematical notation to describe in a precise
way the properties which an information system must have, without
unduly constraining the way in which these properties are achieved.
They describe *what* the system must do without saying *how* it is to be
done. This *abstraction* makes formal specifications useful in the process
of developing a computer system, because they allow questions about

1

what the system does to be answered confidently, without the need to disentangle the information from a mass of detailed program code, or to speculate about the meaning of phrases in an imprecisely-worded prose description.

A formal specification can serve as a single, reliable reference point for those who investigate the customer's needs, those who implement programs to satisfy those needs, those who test the results, and those who write instruction manuals for the system. Because it is independent of the program code, a formal specification of a system can be completed early in its development. Although it might need to be changed as the design team gains in understanding and the perceived needs of the customer evolve, it can be a valuable means of promoting a common understanding among all those concerned with the system.

One way in which mathematical notation can help to achieve these goals is through the use of *mathematical data types* to model the data in a system. These data types are not oriented towards computer representation, but they obey a rich collection of mathematical laws which make it possible to reason effectively about the way a specified system will behave. We use the notation of *predicate logic* to describe abstractly the effect of each operation of our system, again in a way that enables us to reason about its behaviour.

The other main ingredient in Z is a way of decomposing a specification into small pieces called *schemas*. By splitting the specification into schemas, we can present it piece by piece. Each piece can be linked with a commentary which explains informally the significance of the formal mathematics. In Z, schemas are used to describe both static and dynamic aspects of a system. The static aspects include:

- the states it can occupy;

- the invariant relationships that are maintained as the system moves from state to state.

The dynamic aspects include:

- the operations that are possible;

- the relationship between their inputs and outputs;

- the changes of state that happen.

Later, we shall see how the schema language allows different facets of a system to be described separately, then related and combined. For example, the operation of a system when it receives valid input may be described first, then the description may be extended to show how errors in the input are handled. Or the evolution of a single process in a complete system may be described in isolation, then related to the evolution of the system as a whole.

We shall also see how schemas can be used to describe a transformation from one view of a system to another, and so explain why an abstract specification is correctly implemented by another containing more details of a concrete design. By constructing a sequence of specifications, each containing more details than the last, we can eventually arrive at a program with confidence that it satisfies the specification.

1.2 The birthday book

The best way to see how these ideas work out is to look at a small example. For a first example, it is important to choose something simple, and I have chosen a system so simple that it is usually implemented with a notebook and pencil rather than a computer. It is a system which records people's birthdays, and is able to issue a reminder when the day comes round.

In our account of the system, we shall need to deal with people's names and with dates. For present purposes, it will not matter what form these names and dates take, so we introduce the set of all names and the set of all dates as *basic types* of the specification. This allows us to name the sets without saying what kind of objects they contain.

$$[NAME, DATE]$$

The first aspect of the system to describe is its *state space*, and we do this with a schema:

$$
\begin{array}{|l}
\hline
\_BirthdayBook \underline{\hspace{6cm}} \\
known : \mathbb{P}\ NAME \\
birthday : NAME \nrightarrow DATE \\
\hline
known = \mathrm{dom}\ birthday \\
\hline
\end{array}
$$

Like most schemas, this consists of a part above the central dividing line, in which some variables are declared, and a part below the line which gives a relationship between the values of the variables. In this case we are describing the state space of a system, and the two variables represent important *observations* which we can make of the state:

- *known* is the set of names with birthdays recorded;

- *birthday* is a function which, when applied to certain names, gives the birthdays associated with them.

The part of the schema below the line gives a relationship which is true in every state of the system and is maintained by every operation on it: in this case, it says that the set *known* is the same as the domain of the function *birthday* – the set of names to which it can be validly applied. This relationship is an *invariant* of the system.

In this example, the invariant allows the value of the variable *known* to be derived from the value of *birthday*: *known* is a *derived* component of the state, and it would be possible to specify the system without mentioning *known* at all. However, giving names to important concepts helps to make specifications more readable; because we are describing an abstract view of the state space of the birthday book, we can do this without making a commitment to represent *known* explicitly in an implementation.

One possible state of the system is the following:

$$known = \{ \text{John, Mike, Susan} \}$$
$$birthday = \{ \text{John} \mapsto \text{25–Mar,}$$
$$\text{Mike} \mapsto \text{20–Dec,}$$
$$\text{Susan} \mapsto \text{20–Dec} \}$$

Here there are three names known to the system, and the birthday function associates a date with each of them.

Notice that in this description of the state space of the system, we have not been forced to place a limit on the number of birthdays recorded in the birthday book, nor to say that the entries will be stored in a particular order. We have also avoided making a premature decision about the format of names and dates. On the other hand, we have concisely captured the information that each person can have only one birthday, because the variable *birthday* is a function, and that two people can share the same birthday as in our example.

So much for the state space; we can now start on some *operations* on the system. The first of these is to add a new birthday, and we describe it with a schema:

$$
\begin{array}{|l}
\hline
\_AddBirthday _____ \\
\Delta BirthdayBook \\
name? : NAME \\
date? : DATE \\
\hline
name? \notin known \\
birthday' = birthday \cup \{name? \mapsto date?\} \\
\hline
\end{array}
$$

The declaration $\Delta BirthdayBook$ alerts us to the fact that the schema is describing a *state change*: it introduces four variables *known*, *birthday*, *known'* and *birthday'*. The first two are observations of the state before the change, and the last two are observations of the state after the change. Each pair of variables is implicitly constrained to satisfy the invariant, so it must hold both before and after the operation. Next come the declarations of the two inputs to the operation. By convention, the names of inputs end in a question mark.

The part of the schema below the line first of all gives a *precondition* for the success of the operation: the name to be added must not already be one of those known to the system. This is reasonable, since each person can only have one birthday. This specification does not say what happens if the pre-condition is not satisfied: we shall see later how to extend the specification to say that an error message is to be produced. If the pre-condition is satisfied, however, the second line says that the birthday function is extended to map the new name to the given date.

We expect that the set of names known to the system will be augmented with the new name:

$$known' = known \cup \{name?\}$$

In fact we can prove this from the specification of $AddBirthday$, using the invariants on the state before and after the operation:

$known'$

$\quad = \operatorname{dom} birthday'$ [invariant after]

$\quad = \operatorname{dom}(birthday \cup \{name? \mapsto date?\})$ [spec. of $AddBirthday$]

$\quad = \operatorname{dom} birthday \cup \operatorname{dom} \{name? \mapsto date?\}$ [fact about 'dom']

$\quad = \operatorname{dom} birthday \cup \{name?\}$ [fact about 'dom']

$\quad = known \cup \{name?\}$ [invariant before]

Stating and proving properties like this one is a good way of making sure the specification is accurate; reasoning from the specification allows us to explore the behaviour of the system without going to the trouble and expense of implementing it. The two facts about 'dom' used in this proof are examples of the laws obeyed by mathematical data types:

$$\operatorname{dom}(f \cup g) = (\operatorname{dom} f) \cup (\operatorname{dom} g)$$
$$\operatorname{dom}\{a \mapsto b\} = \{a\}$$

Chapter 4 contains many laws like these.

Another operation might be to find the birthday of a person known to the system. Again we describe the operation with a schema:

FindBirthday
$\Xi BirthdayBook$
$name? : NAME$
$date! : DATE$

$name? \in known$
$date! = birthday(name?)$

Two new notations are illustrated by this schema. One is the declaration $\Xi BirthdayBook$, indicating an operation in which the state does not change: the values $known'$ and $birthday'$ of the observations after the operation are equal to their values $known$ and $birthday$ beforehand. Including $\Xi BirthdayBook$ above the line has the same effect as including $\Delta BirthdayBook$ above the line and the two equations:

$$known' = known$$
$$birthday' = birthday$$

below it. The other notation is the use of a name ending in an exclamation mark for an output: the *FindBirthday* operation takes a name as input and yields the corresponding birthday as output. The pre-condition for success of the operation is that $name?$ is one of the names known to the system; if this is so, the output $date!$ is the value of the birthday function at argument $name?$.

The most useful operation on the system is the one to find which people have birthdays on a given date. The operation has one input $today?$, and one output, $cards!$, which is a *set* of names: there may be zero, one, or more people with birthdays on a particular day, to whom birthday cards should be sent.

Remind
$\Xi BirthdayBook$
$today? : DATE$
$cards! : \mathbb{P} \, NAME$

$cards! = \{\, n : known \mid birthday(n) = today? \,\}$

Again the Ξ convention is used to indicate that the state does not change. This time there is no pre-condition. The output $cards!$ is specified to be equal to the set of all values n drawn from the set *known* such that the value of the birthday function at n is $today?$. In general, y is a member of the set $\{\, x : S \mid \ldots x \ldots \,\}$ exactly if y is a member of S and the condition $\ldots y \ldots$, obtained by replacing x with y, is satisfied:

$$y \in \{\, x : S \mid \ldots x \ldots \,\} \Leftrightarrow y \in S \wedge (\ldots y \ldots)$$

So, in our case,

$$m \in \{\, n : known \mid birthday(n) = today? \,\}$$
$$\Leftrightarrow m \in known \wedge birthday(m) = today?$$

A name m is in the output set *cards!* exactly if it is known to the system and the birthday recorded for it is *today?*.

To finish the specification, we must say what state the system is in when it is first started. This is the *initial state* of the system, and it also is specified by a schema:

```
┌─ InitBirthdayBook ─────────────────────────────
│ BirthdayBook
├────────────────────────────────────────────────
│ known = ∅
```

This schema describes a birthday book in which the set *known* is empty: in consequence, the function *birthday* is empty too.

What have we achieved in this specification? We have described in the same mathematical framework both the state space of our birthday-book system and the operations which can be performed on it. The data objects which appear in the system were described in terms of mathematical data types such as sets and functions. The description of the state space included an invariant relationship between the parts of the state – information which would not be part of a program implementing the system, but which is vital to understanding it.

The effects of the operations are described in terms of the relationship which must hold between the input and the output, rather than by giving a recipe to be followed. This is particularly striking in the case of the *Remind* operation, where we simply documented the conditions under which a name should appear in the output. An implementation would probably have to examine the known names one at a time, printing the ones with today's date as it found them, but this complexity has been avoided in the specification. The implementor is free to use this technique, or any other one, as he or she chooses.

1.3 Strengthening the specification

A correct implementation of our specification will faithfully record birthdays and display them, so long as there are no mistakes in the input. But the specification has a serious flaw: as soon as the user tries to add a birthday for someone already known to the system, or tries to find the birthday of someone not known, it says nothing about what happens next. The action of the system may be perfectly reasonable: it may simply ignore the incorrect input. On the other hand, the system may break down: it may start to display rubbish, or perhaps worst of all, it may appear to operate normally for several months, until one day it simply forgets the birthday of a rich and elderly relation.

Does this mean that we should scrap the specification and begin a new one? That would be a shame, because the specification we have describes clearly and concisely the behaviour for correct input, and modifying it to describe the handling of incorrect input could only make it obscure. Luckily there is a better solution: we can describe, separately from the first specification, the errors which might be detected and the desired responses to them, then use the operations of the Z *schema calculus* to combine the two descriptions into a stronger specification.

We shall add an extra output *result!* to each operation on the system. When an operation is successful, this output will take the value *ok*, but it may take the other values *already_known* and *not_known* when an error is detected. The following *free type definition* defines *REPORT* to be a set containing exactly these three values:

$$REPORT ::= ok \mid already\_known \mid not\_known$$

We can define a schema *Success* which just specifies that the result should be *ok*:

$$
\begin{array}{l}
\quad\text{\_\_}Success\text{_____} \\
\quad\mid\; result! : REPORT \\
\quad\text{_____} \\
\quad\mid\; result! = ok \\
\quad\text{_____}
\end{array}
$$

The conjunction operator $\wedge$ of the schema calculus allows us to combine this description with our previous description of *AddBirthday*:

$$AddBirthday \wedge Success$$

This describes an operation which, for correct input, both acts as described by *AddBirthday* and produces the result *ok*.

For each error that might be detected in the input, we define a schema which describes the conditions under which the error occurs and specifies that the appropriate report is produced. Here is a schema which specifies that the report *already_known* should be produced when the input *name?* is already a member of *known*:

```
┌─ AlreadyKnown ─────────────────────────────────
│ ΞBirthdayBook
│ name? : NAME
│ result! : REPORT
├────────────────────────────────────────────────
│ name? ∈ known
│ result! = already_known
└────────────────────────────────────────────────
```

The declaration $\Xi BirthdayBook$ specifies that if the error occurs, the state of the system should not change.

We can combine this description with the previous one to give a specification for a robust version of *AddBirthday*:

$$RAddBirthday \ \hat{=} \ (AddBirthday \wedge Success) \vee AlreadyKnown$$

This definition written with the sign $\hat{=}$ introduces a new schema called *RAddBirthday*, obtained by combining the three schemas shown on the right-hand side. The operation *RAddBirthday* must terminate whatever its input. If the input *name?* is already known, the state of the system does not change, and the result *already_known* is returned; otherwise, the new birthday is added to the database as described by *AddBirthday*, and the result *ok* is returned.

We have specified the various requirements for this operation separately, and then combined them into a single specification of the whole behaviour of the operation. This does not mean that each requirement must be implemented separately, and the implementations combined somehow. In fact, an implementation might search for a place to store the new birthday, and at the same time check that the name is not already known; the code for normal operation and error handling might be thoroughly mingled. This is an example of the abstraction which is possible when we use a specification language free from the constraints necessary in a programming language. The operators ∧ and ∨ cannot (in general) be implemented efficiently as ways of combining programs, but this should not stop us from using them to combine specifications if that is a convenient thing to do.

The operation *RAddBirthday* could be specified directly by writing a single schema which combines the predicate parts of the three constituents *AddBirthday*, *Success* and *AlreadyKnown*:

$\underline{RAddBirthday}$ _____

$\Delta BirthdayBook$
$name? : NAME$
$date? : DATE$
$result! : REPORT$

$(name? \notin known \land$
$\quad birthday' = birthday \cup \{name? \mapsto date?\} \land$
$\quad result! = ok) \lor$
$(name? \in known \land$
$\quad birthday' = birthday \land$
$\quad result! = already\_known)$

As you can see, the effect of the schema $\lor$ operator is to make a schema in which the predicate part is the result of joining the predicate parts of its two arguments with the logical connective $\lor$. Similarly, the effect of the schema $\land$ operator is to take the conjunction of the two predicate parts. Any common variables of the two schemas are merged: in this example, the input $name?$, the output $result!$, and the four observations of the state before and after the operation are shared by the two arguments of $\lor$. In order to write $RAddBirthday$ as a single schema, it has been necessary to write out explicitly something which was implicitly part of the declaration $\Xi BirthdayBook$, namely that the state doesn't change.

A robust version of the $FindBirthday$ operation must be able to report if the input name is not known:

$\underline{NotKnown}$ _____

$\Xi BirthdayBook$
$name? : NAME$
$result! : REPORT$

$name? \notin known$
$result! = not\_known$

The robust operation either behaves as described by $FindBirthday$ and reports success, or reports that the name was not known:

$$RFindBirthday \;\hat{=}\; (FindBirthday \land Success) \lor NotKnown$$

The $Remind$ operation can be called at any time: it never results in an error, so the robust version need only add the reporting of success:

$$RRemind \;\hat{=}\; Remind \land Success$$

The separation of normal operation from error-handling which we have seen here is the simplest but also the most common kind of modularization possible with the schema calculus. More complex modularizations include *promotion* or *framing*, where operations on a single entity – for example, a file – are made into operations on a named entity in a larger system – for example, a named file in a directory. The operations of reading and writing a file might be described by schemas. Separately, another schema might describe the way a file can be accessed in a directory under its name. Putting these two parts together would then result in a specification of operations for reading and writing named files.

Other modularizations are possible: for example, the specification of a system with access restrictions might separate the description of who may call an operation from the description of what the operation actually does. There are also facilities for generic definitions in Z which allow, for example, the notion of resource management to be specified in general, then applied to various aspects of a complex system.

1.4 From specifications to designs

We have seen how the Z notation can be used to specify software modules, and how the schema calculus allows us to put together the specification of a module from pieces which describe various facets of its function. Now we turn our attention to the techniques used in Z to document the design of a program which implements the specification.

The central idea is to describe the concrete data structures which the program will use to represent the abstract data in the specification, and to derive descriptions of the operations in terms of the concrete data structures. We call this process *data refinement*, and it is fully explained in Chapter 5. Often, a data refinement will allow some of the control structure of the program to be made explicit, and this is achieved by one or more steps of *operation refinement* or *algorithm development*.

For simple systems, it is possible to go from the abstract specification to the final program in one step, a method sometimes called *direct refinement*. In more complex systems, however, there are too many design decisions for them all to be recorded clearly in a single refinement step, and the technique of *deferred refinement* is appropriate. Instead of a finished program, the first refinement step results in a new specification, and this is then subjected to further steps of refinement until a program is at last reached. The result is a sequence of design documents, each describing a small collection of related design decisions. As the details of the data structures are filled in step by step, so more of the control structure can be filled in, leaving certain sub-tasks to be implemented in subsequent refinement steps. These sub-tasks can be made into subroutines in the final program, so the step-wise structure of the development leads to a modular structure in the program.

Program developments are often documented by giving an idealized account of the path from specification to program. In these accounts, the ideas all appear miraculously at the right time, one after another. There are no mistakes, no false starts, no decisions taken which are later revised. Of course, real program developments do not happen like that, and the earlier stages of a development are often revised many times as later stages cast new light on the system. In any case, specifications are seldom written without at least a rough idea of how they might be implemented, and it is very rare to find that something similar has not been implemented before. This does not mean that the idealized accounts are worthless, however. They are often the best way of presenting the decisions which have been made and the relationships between them, and such an account can be a valuable piece of documentation.

The rest of this chapter concentrates on data refinement in Z, although the results of the operation refinement which might follow it are shown. Two examples of data refinement are presented. The first shows direct refinement; the birthday book we specified in Section 1.2 is implemented using a pair of arrays. In the second example, deferred refinement is used to show the implementation of a simple checkpoint-restart mechanism. The implementation uses two sub-modules for which specifications in Z are derived as part of the refinement step. This demonstrates the way in which mathematics can help us to explore design decisions at a high level of abstraction.

1.5 Implementing the birthday book

The specification of the birthday book worked with abstract data structures chosen for their expressive clarity rather than their ability to be directly represented in a computer. In the implementation, the data structures must be chosen with an opposite set of criteria, but they can still be modelled with mathematical data types and documented with schemas.

In our implementation, we choose to represent the birthday book with two arrays, which might be declared by

names : **array** [1 ..] **of** *NAME*;
dates : **array** [1 ..] **of** *DATE*;

I have made these arrays 'infinite' for the sake of simplicity. In a real system development, we would use the schema calculus to specify a limit on the number of entries, with appropriate error reports if the limit is exceeded. Finite arrays could then be used in a more realistic implementation; but for now, this would just be a distraction, so let us pretend that potentially infinite arrays are part of our programming language. We shall, in any case, only use a finite part of them at any time.

These arrays can be modelled mathematically by functions from the set N_1 of strictly positive integers to *NAME* or *DATE*:

names : $N_1 \rightarrow NAME$
dates : $N_1 \rightarrow DATE$

The element *names*[*i*] of the array is simply the value *names*(*i*) of the function, and the assignment *names*[*i*] := *v* is exactly described by the specification

$$names' = names \oplus \{i \mapsto v\}$$

The right-hand side of this equation is a function which takes the same value as *names* everywhere except at the argument *i*, where it takes the value *v*.

We describe the state space of the program as a schema. There is another variable *hwm* (for 'high water mark'); it shows how much of the arrays is in use.

_ *BirthdayBook*1 _____
 names : $N_1 \rightarrow NAME$
 dates : $N_1 \rightarrow DATE$
 hwm : N
 ————————————————
 $\forall i, j : 1 .. hwm \bullet$
  $i \neq j \Rightarrow names(i) \neq names(j)$

The predicate part of this schema says that there are no repetitions among the elements *names*(1), ..., *names*(*hwm*).

The idea of this representation is that each name is linked with the date in the corresponding element of the array *dates*. We can document this with a schema *Abs* that defines the *abstraction relation* between the abstract state space *BirthdayBook* and the concrete state space *BirthdayBook*1:

```
┌─ Abs ──────────────────────────────────────────────
│ BirthdayBook
│ BirthdayBook1
├────────────────────────────────────────────────────
│ known = { i : 1 .. hwm • names(i) }
│ ∀ i : 1 .. hwm •
│     birthday(names(i)) = dates(i)
└────────────────────────────────────────────────────
```

This schema relates two points of view on the state of the system. The observations involved are both those of the abstract state – *known* and *birthday* – and those of the concrete state – *names*, *dates* and *hwm*. The first predicate says that the set *known* consists of just those names which occur somewhere among *names*(1), ..., *names*(*hwm*). The set $\{\, y : S \bullet \ldots y \ldots \,\}$ contains those values taken by the expression $\ldots y \ldots$ as y takes values in the set S, so *known* contains a name n exactly if $n = names(i)$ for some value of i such that $1 \le i \le hwm$. We can write this in symbols with an existential quantifier:

$$n \in known \Leftrightarrow (\exists\, i : 1 .. hwm \bullet n = names(i))$$

The second predicate says that the birthday for *names*(*i*) is the corresponding element *dates*(*i*) of the array *dates*.

Having explained what the concrete state space is, and how concrete states are related to abstract states, we can begin to implement the operations of the specification. To add a new name, we increase *hwm* by one, and fill in the name and date in the arrays:

```
┌─ AddBirthday1 ─────────────────────────────────────
│ Δ BirthdayBook1
│ name? : NAME
│ date? : DATE
├────────────────────────────────────────────────────
│ ∀ i : 1 .. hwm • name? ≠ names(i)
│ hwm' = hwm + 1
│ names' = names ⊕ { hwm' ↦ name? }
│ dates' = dates ⊕ { hwm' ↦ date? }
└────────────────────────────────────────────────────
```

This schema describes an operation which has the same inputs and outputs as *AddBirthday*, but operates on the concrete instead of the abstract state. It is a correct implementation of *AddBirthday*, because of the following two facts:

1. Whenever *AddBirthday* is legal in some abstract state, the implementation *AddBirthday1* is legal in any corresponding concrete state.

2. The final state which results from *AddBirthday1* represents an abstract state which *AddBirthday* could produce.

Let us look at the reasons why these two facts are true. The operation *AddBirthday* is legal exactly if its pre-condition $name? \notin known$ is satisfied. If this is so, the predicate

$$known = \{\, i : 1 \mathinner{\ldotp\ldotp} hwm \bullet names(i) \,\}$$

from *Abs* tells us that *name?* is not one of the elements $names(i)$:

$$\forall i : 1 \mathinner{\ldotp\ldotp} hwm \bullet name? \neq names(i)$$

This is the pre-condition of *AddBirthday1*.

To prove the second fact, we need to think about the concrete states before and after an execution of *AddBirthday1*, and the abstract states they represent according to *Abs*. The two concrete states are related by *AddBirthday1*, and we must show that the two abstract states are related as prescribed by *AddBirthday*:

$$birthday' = birthday \cup \{name? \mapsto date?\}$$

The domains of these two functions are the same, because

$$
\begin{aligned}
&\operatorname{dom} birthday' \\
&= known' &&\text{[invariant after]} \\
&= \{\, i : 1 \mathinner{\ldotp\ldotp} hwm' \bullet names'(i) \,\} &&\text{[from } Abs'\text{]} \\
&= \{\, i : 1 \mathinner{\ldotp\ldotp} hwm \bullet names'(i) \,\} \cup \{names'(hwm')\} \\
&&&\text{[since } hwm' = hwm + 1\text{]} \\
&= \{\, i : 1 \mathinner{\ldotp\ldotp} hwm \bullet names(i) \,\} \cup \{name?\} \\
&&&\text{[since } names' = names \oplus \{hwm' \mapsto name?\}\text{]} \\
&= known \cup \{name?\} &&\text{[from } Abs\text{]} \\
&= \operatorname{dom} birthday \cup \{name?\} &&\text{[invariant before]}
\end{aligned}
$$

There is no change in the part of the arrays which was in use before the operation, so for all i in the range $1 \mathinner{\ldotp\ldotp} hwm$,

$$names'(i) = names(i) \wedge dates'(i) = dates(i)$$

For any i in this range,

$$
\begin{aligned}
&birthday'(names'(i)) \\
&= dates'(i) &&\text{[from } Abs'\text{]}
\end{aligned}
$$

$$= dates(i) \qquad\qquad\qquad [dates \text{ unchanged}]$$
$$= birthday(names(i)) \qquad\qquad\qquad [\text{from } Abs]$$

For the new name, stored at index $hwm' = hwm + 1$,

$$birthday'(names'(hwm'))$$
$$= dates'(hwm') \qquad\qquad\qquad [\text{from } Abs']$$
$$= date? \qquad\qquad\qquad [\text{spec. of } AddBirthday1]$$

So the two functions $birthday'$ and $birthday \cup \{name? \mapsto date?\}$ are equal, and the abstract states before and after the operation are guaranteed to be related as described by $AddBirthday$.

The description of the concrete operation uses only notation which has a direct counterpart in our programming language, so we can translate it directly into a subroutine to perform the operation:

procedure $AddBirthday(name : NAME; \; date : DATE)$;
begin
    $hwm := hwm + 1$;
    $names[hwm] := name$;
    $dates[hwm] := date$
end;

The second operation, $FindBirthday$, is implemented by the following operation, again described in terms of the concrete state:

```
┌─ FindBirthday1 ──────────────────────────
│ ΞBirthdayBook1
│ name? : NAME
│ date! : DATE
├──────────────────────────────────────────
│ ∃ i : 1 .. hwm •
│     name? = names(i) ∧ date! = dates(i)
└──────────────────────────────────────────
```

The predicate says that there is an index i at which the $names$ array contains the input $name?$, and the output $date!$ is the corresponding element of the array $dates$. For this to be possible, $name?$ must in fact appear somewhere in the array $names$: this is the pre-condition of the operation.

Since neither the abstract nor the concrete operation changes the state, there is no need to check that the final concrete state is acceptable, but we need to check that the pre-condition of $FindBirthday1$ is sufficiently liberal, and that the output $date!$ is correct. The pre-conditions of the abstract and concrete operations are in fact the same:

that the input *name?* is known. The output is correct because for some i, *name?* = *names(i)* and *date!* = *dates(i)*, so

date!

= *dates(i)*	[spec. of *FindBirthday1*]
= *birthday(names(i))*	[from *Abs*]
= *birthday(name?)*	[spec. of *FindBirthday1*]

The existential quantifier in the description of *FindBirthday1* leads to a loop in the program code, searching for a suitable value of i:

> **procedure** *FindBirthday*(*name* : *NAME*; **var** *date* : *DATE*);
>   **var** i : *INTEGER*;
> **begin**
> $i := 1$;
>   **while** *names*[i] $\neq$ *name* **do** $i := i + 1$;
>   *date* := *dates*[i]
> **end**;

The operation *Remind* poses a new problem, because its output *cards* is a *set* of names, and cannot be directly represented in the programming language. We can deal with it by introducing a new abstraction relation, showing how it can be represented by an array and an integer:

> *AbsCards* _____
> *cards* : $\mathbb{P}$ *NAME*
> *cardlist* : $\mathbb{N}_1 \rightarrow$ *NAME*
> *ncards* : $\mathbb{N}$
> _____
> *cards* = $\{ i : 1 .. \ ncards \bullet cardlist(i) \}$

The concrete operation can now be described: it produces as outputs *cardlist* and *ncards*:

> *Remind1* _____
> Ξ*BirthdayBook1*
> *today?* : *DATE*
> *cardlist!* : $\mathbb{N}_1 \rightarrow$ *NAME*
> *ncards!* : $\mathbb{N}$
> _____
> $\{ i : 1 .. \ ncards! \bullet cardlist!(i) \}$
>   = $\{ j : 1 .. \ hwm \mid dates(j) = today? \bullet names(j) \}$

The set on the right-hand side of the equation contains all the names in the *names* array for which the corresponding entry in the *dates* array is *today?*. The program code for *Remind* uses a loop to examine the entries one by one:

```
procedure Remind(today : DATE;
                      var cardlist : array [1 .. ] of NAME;
                      var ncards : INTEGER);
    var j : INTEGER;
begin
    ncards := 0; j := 0;
    while j < hwm do begin
        j := j + 1;
        if dates[j] = today then begin
            ncards := ncards + 1;
            cardlist[ncards] := names[j]
        end
    end
end;
```

The initial state of the program has $hwm = 0$:

```
┌─ InitBirthdayBook1 ─────────────────────────
│  BirthdayBook1
│ ──────────────────────────────────────
│  hwm = 0
└─────────────────────────────────────────
```

Nothing is said about the initial values of the arrays *names* and *dates*, because they do not matter. If the initial concrete state satisfies this description, and it is related to the initial abstract state by the abstraction schema *Abs*, then

$$known$$
$$= \{ i : 1 .. hwm \bullet names(i) \} \qquad \text{[from } Abs \text{]}$$
$$= \{ i : 1 .. 0 \bullet names(i) \} \qquad \text{[from } InitBirthdayBook1 \text{]}$$
$$= \varnothing \qquad \text{[since } 1 .. 0 = \varnothing \text{]}$$

so the initial abstract state is as described by *InitBirthdayBook*. This description of the initial concrete state can be used to write a subroutine to initialize our program module:

```
procedure InitBirthdayBook;
begin
    hwm := 0
end;
```

In this direct refinement, we have taken the birthday book specification and in a single step produced a program module which implements it. The relationship between the state of the book as described in the specification and the values of the program variables which represent that state was documented with an abstraction schema, and this allowed descriptions of the operations in terms of the program variables to be be derived. These operations were simple enough to implement immediately, but in a more complex example, rules of operation refinement could be used to check the code against the concrete operation descriptions.

1.6 A simple checkpointing scheme

This example shows how refinement techniques can be used at a high level in the design of systems, as well as in detailed programming. What we shall call a *database* is simply a function from addresses to pages of data. We first introduce *ADDR* and *PAGE* as basic types:

$$[ADDR, PAGE]$$

We can define *DATABASE* as an abbreviation for the set of all functions from *ADDR* to *PAGE*, using the definition sign ==:

$$DATABASE == ADDR \rightarrow PAGE$$

We shall be looking at a system which – from the user's point of view – contains two versions of a database. Here is a schema describing the state-space:

```
┌─ CheckSys ─────────────────────────────────────
│ working : DATABASE
│ backup : DATABASE
└─────────────────────────────────────────────────
```

This schema has no predicate part: it specifies that the two observations *working* and *backup* may be any databases at all, and need not be related in any way.

Most operations affect only the working database. For example, it is possible to access the page at a specified address:

```
┌─ Access ───────────────────────────────────────
│ Ξ CheckSys
│ a? : ADDR
│ p! : PAGE
│ ────────────────────────────────────────────────
│ p! = working(a?)
└─────────────────────────────────────────────────
```

This operation takes an address $a?$ as input, and produces as its output $p!$ the page stored in the working database at that address. Neither version of the database changes in the operation.

It is also possible to update the working database with a new page:

```
┌─ Update ──────────────────────────────────────
│ ΔCheckSys
│ a? : ADDR
│ p? : PAGE
├───────────────────────────────────────────────
│ working' = working ⊕ {a? ↦ p?}
│ backup' = backup
└───────────────────────────────────────────────
```

In this operation, both an address $a?$ and a page $p?$ are supplied as input, and the working database is updated so that the page $p?$ is now stored at address $a?$. The page previously stored at address $a?$ is lost.

There are two operations involving the back-up database. We can take a copy of the working database: this is the *CheckPoint* operation:

```
┌─ CheckPoint ──────────────────────────────────
│ ΔCheckSys
├───────────────────────────────────────────────
│ working' = working
│ backup' = working
└───────────────────────────────────────────────
```

We can also restore the working database to the state it had at the last checkpoint:

```
┌─ Restart ─────────────────────────────────────
│ ΔCheckSys
├───────────────────────────────────────────────
│ working' = backup
│ backup' = backup
└───────────────────────────────────────────────
```

This completes the specification of our system, and we can begin to think of how we might implement it. A first idea might be really to keep two copies of the database, so implementing the specification directly. But experience tells us that copying the entire database is an expensive operation, and that if checkpoints are taken frequently, then the computer will spend much more time copying than it does accessing and updating the working database.

A better idea for an implementation might be to keep only one complete copy of the database, together with a record of the changes made since creation of this master copy. The master copy consists of a single database:

```
┌─ Master ──────────────────────────────────────────────
│ master : DATABASE
└───────────────────────────────────────────────────────
```

The record of changes made since the last checkpoint is a *partial function* from addresses to pages: it is partial because we expect that not every page will have been updated since the last checkpoint.

```
┌─ Changes ─────────────────────────────────────────────
│ changes : ADDR ⇸ PAGE
└───────────────────────────────────────────────────────
```

The concrete state space is described by putting these two parts together:

```
┌─ CheckSys1 ───────────────────────────────────────────
│ Master
│ Changes
└───────────────────────────────────────────────────────
```

How does this concrete state space mirror our original abstract view? The master database is what we described as the back-up, and the working database is $master \oplus changes$, the result of updating the master copy with the recorded changes. We can record this relationship with an abstraction schema:

```
┌─ Abs ─────────────────────────────────────────────────
│ CheckSys
│ CheckSys1
│ ──────────────────────────────────────────────────────
│ backup = master
│ working = master ⊕ changes
└───────────────────────────────────────────────────────
```

The notation $master \oplus changes$ denotes a function which agrees with *master* everywhere except in the domain of *changes*, where it agrees with *changes*.

How can we implement the four operations? Accessing a page at address $a?$ should return $working(a?) = (master \oplus changes)(a?)$, so a valid specification of *Access1* is as follows:

```
┌─ Access1 ─────────────────────────────────────────────
│ ΞCheckSys1
│ a? : ADDR
│ p! : PAGE
│ ──────────────────────────────────────────────────────
│ p! = (master ⊕ changes)(a?)
└───────────────────────────────────────────────────────
```

But we can do a little better than this: if $a? \in \text{dom } changes$, then

$$(master \oplus changes)(a?) = changes(a?)$$

and if $a? \notin \text{dom } changes$, then

$$(master \oplus changes)(a?) = master(a?)$$

So we can use operation refinement to develop the operation further; it is implemented by

procedure *Access*($a : ADDR$; **var** $p : PAGE$);
    var $r : REPORT$;
begin
    GetChange(a, p, r);
    if $r \neq ok$ **then**
        ReadMaster(a, p)
end;

What are the operations *GetChange* and *ReadMaster*? We need give only their specifications here, and can leave their implementation to a later stage in the development. *GetChange* operates only on the *changes* part of the state; it checks whether a given page is present, returning a report and, if possible, the page itself:

    ┌─ *GetChange* ─────────────────────
    │ $\Xi Changes$
    │ $a? : ADDR$
    │ $p! : PAGE$
    │ $r! : REPORT$
    ├──────────────────────────────
    │ $(a? \in \text{dom } changes \land$
    │ $p! = changes(a?) \land$
    │ $r! = ok) \lor$
    │ $(a? \notin \text{dom } changes \land$
    │ $r! = not\_present)$
    └──────────────────────────────

As you will see, this is a specification which could be structured nicely with the schema $\lor$ operator. The *ReadMaster* operation simply returns a page from the *master* database:

    ┌─ *ReadMaster* ─────────────────────
    │ $\Xi Master$
    │ $a? : ADDR$
    │ $p! : PAGE$
    ├──────────────────────────────
    │ $p! = master(a?)$
    └──────────────────────────────

For the *Update* operation, we want $backup' = backup$, so

$$master' = backup' = backup = master$$

Also $working' = working \oplus \{a? \mapsto p?\}$, so we want

$$master' \oplus changes' = (master \oplus changes) \oplus \{a? \mapsto p?\}$$

Luckily, the overriding operator $\oplus$ is associative: it satisfies the law

$$(f \oplus g) \oplus h = f \oplus (g \oplus h)$$

If we let $changes' = changes \oplus \{a? \mapsto p?\}$, then

$$
\begin{aligned}
working' \\
&= working \oplus \{a? \mapsto p?\} && \text{[spec. of } Updaie] \\
&= (master \oplus changes) \oplus \{a? \mapsto p?\} && \text{[from } Abs] \\
&= master \oplus (changes \oplus \{a? \mapsto p?\}) && \text{[associativity of } \oplus] \\
&= master' \oplus changes' && \text{[spec. of } Update1]
\end{aligned}
$$

and the abstraction relation is maintained. So the specification for *Update*1 is

```
┌─ Update1 ─────────────────────────────────
│ ΔCheckSys1
│ a? : ADDR
│ p? : PAGE
├────────────────────────────────────────────
│ master' = master
│ changes' = changes ⊕ {a? ↦ p?}
└────────────────────────────────────────────
```

This is implemented by an operation *MakeChange* which has the same effect as described here, but operates only on the *Changes* part of the state.

For the *CheckPoint* operation, we want $backup' = working$, so we immediately see that

$$master' = backup' = working = master \oplus changes$$

We also want $working' = working$, so

$$master' \oplus changes' = master \oplus changes = master'$$

This equation is solved by setting $changes' = \varnothing$, since the empty function $\varnothing$ is a right identity for $\oplus$, as expressed by the law

$$f \oplus \varnothing = f$$

So a specification for *CheckPoint*1 is

CheckPoint1 _____

$\Delta CheckSys1$

$master' = master \oplus changes$

$changes' = \varnothing$

_____

This can be refined to the code

    MultiWrite(*changes*); *ResetChanges*

where *MultiWrite* performs the updating of the *master* database, and *ResetChanges* sets *changes* to $\varnothing$.

    Finally, for the operation *Restart1*, we have $backup' = backup$, so we need $master' = master$, as for *Update*. Again, we want

$$master' \oplus changes' = master'$$

this time because $working' = backup$, so we choose $changes' = \varnothing$ as before:

Restart1 _____

$\Delta CheckSys1$

$master' = master$

$changes' = \varnothing$

_____

This can be refined to a simple call to *ResetChanges*.

    Now we have found implementations for all the operations of our original specification. In these implementations, we have used two new sets of operations, which we have specified with schemas but not yet implemented. One set, *ReadMaster* and *MultiWrite*, operates on the *master* part of the concrete state, and the other, containing *MakeChange*, *GetChange*, and *ResetChanges*, operates only on the *changes* part of the state. The result is two new specifications for what are in effect modules of the system, and in later stages they can be developed independently. Perhaps the *master* function would be represented by an array of pages stored on a disk, and *changes* by a hash table held in main store.

    The mathematical method can describe data structures with equal ease, whether they are held in primary or secondary storage. It describes operations in terms of their function, and it makes no difference whether the execution takes microseconds or hours to finish. Of course, the designer must be very closely concerned with the capabilities of the equipment to be used, and it is vital to distinguish primary storage, which though fast has limited capacity, from the slower but larger secondary storage. But we regard it as a strength and not a weakness of the mathematical method that it does not reflect this distinction. By modelling only the functional characteristics of a software module, a mathematical specification technique encourages a healthy *separation of concerns*: it helps the designer to focus his or her attention on functional aspects, and to compare different designs, even if they differ widely in performance.

The rest of this book is a reference manual for the notation and ideas used in the examples we have looked at here. In Chapter 2, an outline is given of the mathematical world of sets, relations and functions in which Z operates, and the way Z specifications describe objects in this world. These concepts are applied in Chapter 3, where an account of the Z language is given. The language is made usable by the library of definitions which is implicitly a part of every Z specification, described in Chapter 4 on 'the mathematical tool-kit'. This chapter contains many laws of the kind we have used in reasoning about the examples. Chapter 5 covers the conventions by which Z specifications are used to describe sequential programs, and the rules for developing concrete representations of data types from their mathematical specifications. The final chapter contains a summary of the syntax of the Z language described in the manual.

CHAPTER TWO

Background

Z specifications are mathematical: the variables which appear in them range over mathematical objects, and they express mathematical models of information systems. This chapter contains a description of the world of mathematical objects in which Z specifications have their meaning: it describes what objects there are, and how relationships between them may be made into specifications.

These two themes are developed more fully in later chapters: Chapter 3 deals in detail with the Z language and how it can be used to express specifications, and Chapter 4 extends the vocabulary of mathematical objects into a collection of powerful data types, using the Z language for the definitions.

2.1 Objects and types

Every mathematical expression which appears in a Z specification is given a *type*: this determines a set known to contain the value of the expression. Each variable is given a type by its declaration, and there are rules for deriving the type of each kind of compound expression from the types of its sub-expressions.

Types are important because it is possible to calculate automatically the types of all the expressions in a specification and check that they make sense: for example, in the equation

$$(0, 1) = \{1, 2, 3\}$$

the left-hand side is an ordered pair, but the right-hand side is a set, so in Z the equation is nonsense: this is the kind of mistake which can be detected by a type checker. There is, of course, no guarantee that a specification free from type errors can be implemented, and still less that it really says what the customer wants.

Every Z specification begins with certain objects which play a part in the specification, but have no internal structure of interest. These atomic objects are the members of the *basic types* or *given sets* of the specification. Many specifications have the integers as atomic objects, and these are members of the basic type $\mathbb{Z}$, but there may be other basic types; for example, a specification of a filing system might have file-names as atomic objects belonging to the basic type *FNAME*, and a specification of a language might have expressions as atomic objects belonging to the basic type *EXP*.

From these atomic objects, composite objects can be put together in various ways. These composite objects are the members of composite types put together with the type constructors of Z. There are three kinds of composite types: set types, Cartesian product types, and schema types. The type constructors can be applied repeatedly to obtain more and more complex types, whose members have a more and more complex internal structure.

2.1.1 Sets and set types

Any set of objects of the same type t is itself an object with the *set type* $\mathbb{P}\ t$. Sets may be written in Z by listing their elements. For example:

$$\{1, 2, 4, 8, 16\}$$

has type $\mathbb{P}\ \mathbb{Z}$ and is a set of integers. They may also be written by giving a property which is characteristic of the elements of the set. For example:

$$\{\, p : PERSON \mid age(p) \geq 16 \,\}$$

has type $\mathbb{P}\ PERSON$; it is the set whose members are exactly those members of the basic type *PERSON* for which the function *age* has value at least 16. Two sets of the same type $\mathbb{P}\ t$ are equal exactly if they have the same members.

2.1.2 Tuples and Cartesian product types

If x and y are two objects of types t and u respectively, then the ordered pair (x, y) is an object with the *Cartesian product type* $t \times u$.

Similarly, if x, y and z are three objects of types t, u and v respectively, then the ordered triple (x, y, z) is an object with type $t \times u \times v$.

More generally, if x_1, ..., x_n are n objects of types t_1, ..., t_n respectively, then the ordered n-tuple $(x_1, \ldots, x_n)$ is an object of type $t_1 \times \cdots \times t_n$. If $(y_1, \ldots, y_n)$ is another n-tuple of the same type, then the two are equal exactly if $x_i = y_i$ for each i with $1 \leq i \leq n$.

Note that there is no connection between Cartesian products with different numbers of terms: for example, the ternary product $t \times u \times v$ and is different from the iterated binary products $t \times (u \times v)$ and $(t \times u) \times v$: it is best to think of $t \times u \times v$ as an application of the type constructor $\_ \times \_ \times \_$ of three arguments. Consequently, the triple (a, b, c) is different from both $(a, (b, c))$ and $((a, b), c)$: in fact, they have different types. This distinction allows the application of functions of several arguments to be type-checked more closely. Although in theory it is possible to have tuples with no components or only one component, there is no way to write them in Z specifications.

2.1.3 Bindings and schema types

If p and q are distinct identifiers, and x and y are objects of types t and u respectively, then there is a *binding* z with components $z.p$ equal to x and $z.q$ equal to y. This binding is an object with the *schema type* $\langle\!\langle p : t; \ q : u \rangle\!\rangle$. More generally, if p_1, ..., p_n are distinct identifiers and x_1, ..., x_n are objects of types t_1, ..., t_n respectively, then there is a binding z with components $z.p_i = x_i$ for each i with $1 \leq i \leq n$. This binding is an object with the schema type

$$\langle\!\langle p_1 : t_1; \ \ldots; \ p_n : t_n \rangle\!\rangle$$

The binding z is equal to another binding w of the same type exactly if $z.p_i = w.p_i$ for each i with $1 \leq i \leq n$. Two schema types are regarded as identical if they differ only in the order in which the components are listed.

Bindings are used in the operations of Z which allow instances of a schema to be regarded as mathematical objects: the components of the binding correspond to the components of the schema. Although the notation for schema types is not part of the Z language in the way $\mathbb{P}$ and $\times$ are, the concept is implicit in the operations on schemas provided by the language. The expression θS, where S is a schema, has a binding as its value, and variables with schema types are introduced by declarations like $x : S$ where, again, S is a schema.

2.1.4 Relations and functions

The three kinds of object introduced so far – sets, tuples and bindings – are the only ones which are fundamental to Z. Other mathematical objects can be modelled by combining these three basic constructions, and Chapter 4 contains definitions which accomplish this modelling for several important classes of object.

Among the most important mathematical objects are binary relations and functions, and both are modelled in Z by their *graphs*. The graph of a binary relation is the set of ordered pairs for which it holds: for example, the graph of the relation $\_ < \_$ on integers contains the pairs $(0,1)$, $(0,2)$, $(1,2)$, $(-37,42)$, and so on, but not $(3,3)$ or $(45,34)$. The identification between a binary relation and its graph is so strong in Z that we usually speak of them as being the same object. The notation $X \leftrightarrow Y$, meaning the set of binary relations between the sets X and Y, is defined in Chapter 4 as a synonym for the set $\mathbb{P}(X \times Y)$ of subsets of the set $X \times Y$ of ordered pairs.

Mathematical functions are regarded as a special kind of relation: those which relate each object on the left to at most one object on the right. Chapter 4 defines the notation $X \nrightarrow Y$ as a synonym for the set of relations with this property. They are called *partial* functions, because they need not give a result for every possible argument. The set $X \rightarrow Y$ contains all the *total* functions from X to Y: they relate each member of X to exactly one member of Y. The notation $f(x)$ can be used if f is a function: the value of this expression is that unique element of Y to which f relates x. Functions with several arguments are modelled by letting the set on the left of the arrow be a Cartesian product: in a sense, they do not have many arguments, but only one, which happens to be a tuple.

In common with ordinary mathematical practice, Z regards functions as static relations between arguments and results; this contrasts with the view encouraged by some programming languages, where 'functions' are methods for computing the result from the argument. In particular, we can talk quite freely in Z about two functions being equal – it simply means that they contain the same ordered pairs – even though it is difficult to decide whether two algorithms compute the same result from the same argument, and in general it is impossible to tell. Mathematical functions are a valuable tool for describing data abstractly, even though they cannot be represented directly in the memory of a computer. In the implementation of a specification which talks about functions, design decisions will have to be taken about how the data modelled by functions is to be represented, but the specification abstracts from this detail. The birthday book specification in Chapter 1 used a function *birthday* to model the relationship between names and birthdays; later, the implementation used a pair of arrays to represent the same information. This use of functions in specifications can be compared to the use of real numbers to specify numerical calculations. Even though they cannot be represented exactly by computers, real numbers provide a convenient language for describing calculations which the computer will carry out approximately.

To make the system of types simple enough for types to be calculated automatically, it is necessary to disregard some of the information given in the declaration of a function when calculating its type. In fact, the type system makes no distinction between functions and simple binary relations; the two variables f and g declared by

$$f : A \leftrightarrow B$$
$$g : A \rightarrow B$$

have the same type, namely $\mathbb{P}(A \times B)$. This is because functions are just relations with a certain property, so f could in fact be a function, perhaps by virtue of its definition. So the equation $f = g$ makes perfect sense, and if f is indeed a function, the expression $f(a)$ also makes sense. Deciding whether the definition of f makes it a function is, in general, as difficult as arbitrary theorem-proving, so we cannot expect an automatic type checker to do it for us.

2.2 Properties and schemas

A *signature* is a collection of variable names, each with a type. Signatures are created by declarations, and they provide a vocabulary for making mathematical statements, which are expressed by *predicates*. For example, the declaration $x, y : \mathsf{Z}$ creates a signature with two variables x and y, both of type Z. In this signature, the predicate $x < y$ expresses the property that the value of x is less than the value of y. This will be so when x and y take certain values – if, say, x is 3 and y is 5 – and not when they take certain other values – if, say, x is 6 and y is 4. Two different predicates may express the same property: in the example, the predicate $y > x$ expresses the same property as $x < y$.

Given a signature, we can think of various *situations*, in which the variables take different values drawn from their types. (Situations are called 'assignments', 'interpretations' or 'structures' in mathematical logic; I have avoided these terms because of their different connotations in computing science.) A *property* over the signature is characterized by the situations in which it is true. A predicate expresses a property, and by extension we say a predicate is true in a situation if the property it expresses is true in that situation. We say that the situation *satisfies* the property, or the predicate which expresses it, if the property is true in the situation.

As we have just seen, there may be more than one way of expressing a property as a predicate: we say two predicates in a signature are *logically equivalent* if they express the same property, that is, if one is true in exactly the situations which make the other one true.

A *schema* is a signature together with a property over the signature; the schema *Aleph* with the signature and property in our example might be written

```
┌─ Aleph ──────────────────────────────
│  x, y : Z
│ ─────────────────────────────────────
│  x < y
└──────────────────────────────────────
```

We call x and y the *components* of *Aleph*. For the moment, we may think of the components of a schema as being simply the variables in its signature. Later (in Section 2.3.2) we shall revise this definition to bring global variables into the account. Roughly speaking, the signature and property parts of a schema correspond to the declaration and predicate written in the text of the schema. Sometimes, however, the declaration contributes something to the property; for example, in the schema

```
┌─ Beth ───────────────────────────────
│  f : Z → Z
│ ─────────────────────────────────────
│  f(3) = 4
└──────────────────────────────────────
```

the type of f is $\mathbb{P}(Z \times Z)$, and the fact that f is a function is part of the property, as well as the fact that its value at 3 is 4. We call the property expressed in a declaration the *constraint* of the declaration.

2.2.1 Combining properties

The simplest predicates are *true*, which expresses a property true in all situations, and *false*, which expresses a property true in no situation. An equation

$$E_1 = E_2$$

expresses the property that the values of the expressions E_1 and E_2 are equal, and the predicate

$$E_1 \in E_2$$

expresses the property that the value of E_1 is a member of whatever set is the value of E_2.

These basic predicates can be combined in various ways to express more complicated properties. For example, the predicate

$$P_1 \wedge P_2$$

expresses the *conjunction* of the properties expressed by the predicates P_1 and P_2. It is true exactly when both P_1 and P_2 are true individually. The other connectives of the propositional calculus, $\vee \Rightarrow \neg \Leftrightarrow$, may also be used to combine predicates (see Section 3.7).

If x is a natural number, the *universally quantified* predicate

$$\forall z : \mathsf{N} \bullet x \leq z$$

expresses the property that the value of x is less than or equal to every natural number, i.e. that x is zero. The existential quantifier $\exists$ and the unique quantifier $\exists_1$ may be used as well as $\forall$. The most general form of a universally quantified predicate is

$$\forall D \mid P \bullet Q$$

where D is a declaration and P and Q are predicates. D and P together form a schema S, and the whole predicate expresses the following property: that whatever values are taken by the components of S, if the property of S is satisfied, then the predicate Q will also be satisfied. The components of S are *local variables* of the whole predicate, in a sense explained in Section 2.3.

2.2.2 Decorations

A fundamental operation on schemas is *systematic decoration*. If S is a schema, then S' is the same as S, except that all the component names have been suffixed with the decoration $'$. The signature of S' contains a component x' for each component x of S, and the type of x' in S' is the same as the type of x in S. The property of S' is true in a situation exactly if the property of S is true when each component x takes the value taken by x' in that situation.

There are three standard decorations used in describing operations (see Chapter 5): $'$ for labelling the final state of an operation, $?$ for labelling its inputs, and ! for labelling its outputs. Subscript digits may also be used as decorations. An identifier or schema may have a sequence of decorations, so the identifiers x'', x''', etc. are allowed, as well as the less useful $x'?$, $x?!$, and so on. Note that the identifiers $x_1!$ and $x!_1$ are different.

2.2.3 Combining schemas

Two signatures are said to be *type compatible* if each variable common to the two has the same type in each of them. If two signatures have this property, we can *join* them to make a larger signature which contains all the variables from both of them. For example, the two signatures

$a : \mathbb{P}\, X;\ b : X \times Y$

and

$b : X \times Y;\ c : Z$

are type compatible because their only common variable, namely b, has the same type $X \times Y$ in both of them. They can be joined to make the signature

$a : \mathbb{P}\, X;\ b : X \times Y;\ c : Z$

The new signature contains all the variables of both the original ones, with the same types; for this reason, we say that the original signatures are *sub-signatures* of the new one. If one signature is a sub-signature of another one, a situation for the first can be derived from any situation for the second by simply ignoring the extra variables: we call this situation a *restriction* of the original situation to the smaller signature. Conversely, we say the original situation is an *extension* of this new situation to the larger signature.

To be type compatible, two signatures must give the same type to their common variables, but this does not mean that the variables must be declared in the same way, for as we have seen, a declaration can provide more information than just the type of a variable. As a simple example, both binary relations between two sets X and Y and functions from X to Y have the same type $\mathbb{P}(X \times Y)$, so two signatures would be type compatible even if one resulted from the declaration

$f : X \leftrightarrow Y$

and the other from the declaration

$f : X \rightarrow Y$

Two schemas S and T with type compatible signatures may be combined with the schema conjunction operator to give a new schema $S \wedge T$. The signature of this new schema is the result of joining the signatures of S and T, and its property is in effect the conjunction of the properties of S and T: it is true in any situation exactly if *both* the restriction of the situation to the signature of S satisfies the property of S *and* its restriction to the signature of T satisfies the property of T.

Provided that no component of S has the same name as a global variable mentioned in the body of T, and vice versa (see Section 2.3.2), the schema $S \wedge T$ can be expanded textually: the declaration part of the expansion has all the declarations from both S and T (with duplicates eliminated), and the predicate part is the conjunction of the predicate parts of S and T. For example, if schema *Aleph* is as before, and *Gimel* is defined by

---
Gimel

$y : \mathbb{Z}$
$z : 1 .. 10$

$y = z * z$

---

then *Aleph* $\wedge$ *Gimel* is the schema

$x, y : \mathbb{Z}$
$z : 1 .. 10$

$x < y \wedge y = z * z$

Other logical connectives such as $\vee$, $\Rightarrow$, and $\Leftrightarrow$ may also be used to combine two type compatible schemas. They join the signatures as for $\wedge$, and combine the properties in a way which depends on the connective: for example, the property of $S \vee T$ is true in any situation exactly if either or both of its restrictions are true in S or T. The negation $\neg\, S$ of a schema S has the same signature as S but the negation of its property.

Compound schemas resulting from these operations can also be expanded, but care is necessary if the declaration part contributes to the property of the schema. For example, the negation of the schema *Gimel* defined above is

---
$y, z : \mathbb{Z}$

$z < 1 \vee z > 10 \vee$
$y \neq z * z$

This expansion of ¬ *Gimel* is reached by first making explicit the contribution made by the declaration part of *Gimel* to its property:

┌─ *Gimel* ─────────────────────────────
│ $y, z : \mathsf{Z}$
├───────────────────────────────────────
│ $1 \leq z \leq 10 \;\wedge$
│ $y = z * z$
└───────────────────────────────────────

Only when this information is made explicit can the predicate part be negated directly.

The hiding operators \ and ↾ provide ways of removing components from schemas. If S is a schema, and x_1, ..., x_n are components of S then

$$S \setminus (x_1, \ldots, x_n)$$

is a schema. Its components are the components of S, except for x_1, ..., x_n, and they have the same types as in S. The property of this schema is true in exactly those situations which are a restriction of a situation which satisfies the property of S. If there is no clash of variables, the schema can be written using an existential quantifier: if *Gimel* is the schema defined above, then $Gimel \setminus (z)$ is the schema

┌───────────────────────────────────────
│ $y : \mathsf{Z}$
├───────────────────────────────────────
│ $\exists z : 1 \mathinner{.\,.} 10 \bullet y = z * z$
└───────────────────────────────────────

It is possible (but not very useful) to hide all the components of a schema: the result is a schema with an empty signature and a property which is either always true or always false.

If S and T are schemas with type compatible signatures, then $S \restriction T$ is also a schema: it has the signature of T, and its property is satisfied by exactly those situations which are a restriction of a situation satisfying the property of $S \wedge T$. It is the same as $(S \wedge T) \setminus (x_1, \ldots, x_n)$, where x_1, ..., x_n are all the components of S not shared by T.

Quantifiers provide another way of hiding components of schemas. If D is a declaration, P is a predicate, and S is a schema, then

$$\forall D \mid P \bullet S$$

is a schema. The schema S must have as components all the variables introduced by D, and they must have the same types. The signature of the result contains all the components of S except those introduced by D, and they have the same types as in S. The property of the result is derived as follows: for any situation for the signature of the result, consider all its extensions to the signature of S. If every such extension which satisfies both the constraint of D and the predicate P also satisfies the property of S, then the original situation satisfies the property of $\forall D \mid P \bullet S$.

The schema $\exists D \mid P \bullet S$ has the same signature as $\forall D \mid P \bullet S$, but its property is true in any situation if at least one of its extensions simultaneously satisfies the constraint of D, the predicate P, and the property of S. Similarly, the schema $\exists_1 D \mid P \bullet S$ has the same signature, but its property is true in any situation which can be extended in exactly one way so that these three are simultaneously satisfied.

Quantified schema expressions can be expanded textually by introducing a quantifier into the body of the schema. As an example, the expression

$$\forall z : Z \mid z > 5 \bullet \textit{Gimel}$$

can be written as

$$\begin{array}{|l}
\hline
y : Z \\
\hline
\forall z : Z \mid z > 5 \bullet \\
\quad z \in 1 \mathinner{.\,.} 10 \wedge y = z * z \\
\hline
\end{array}$$

Again, it has been necessary to make explicit the information about z given by its declaration before making the expansion.

2.3 Variables and scope

Specifications can contain both global variables and components of schemas, as well as local variables introduced, for example, by the universal quantifier $\forall$. It is the purpose of the *scope rules* to define the collection of names which may be used at each point in the specification, and to identify the variable to which a name refers at each point.

2.3.1 Nested scopes

Like many programming languages (e.g. Algol 60, Pascal) and many formal systems (e.g. λ-calculus, first-order logic), Z has a system of *nested scopes*. For each variable name introduced by a declaration, there is a region of the specification, called the *scope* of the variable, where the name refers to the variable. We say that the variable is *local* to this region of the specification.

In many cases, the names of variables which are local to a region in a specification can be changed without affecting the meaning: for example, in the predicate

$$\exists\, y : \mathsf{N} \bullet x > y$$

the name of the variable y can be changed without changing the property being expressed; this predicate is logically equivalent to the predicate

$$\exists\, u : \mathsf{N} \bullet x > u$$

The renaming of the local or bound variables of a universally quantified predicate is possible because the names themselves are not part of the meaning of the predicate: we only care about which situations make it true.

Sometimes the scope of a variable has 'holes' in it, caused by a nested declaration of another variable with the same name. For example, in the predicate

$$\exists\, x : \mathsf{N} \bullet ((\exists\, x : \mathsf{N} \bullet x < 10) \wedge x > 3)$$

the occurrence of x in $x < 10$ refers to the inner declaration of x: the whole of the inner quantification is a hole in the scope of the variable x introduced by the outer quantifier. Where renaming of bound variables is possible, this kind of confusion can be avoided, and it is usually good practice to do so: our example might be rewritten as

$$\exists\, x : \mathsf{N} \bullet ((\exists\, y : \mathsf{N} \bullet y < 10) \wedge x > 3)$$

by renaming the bound variable of the inner quantifier, or even – since the inner quantification is now independent of x – as

$$\exists\, x : \mathsf{N} \bullet ((\exists\, y : \mathsf{N} \bullet y < 10) \wedge x > 3)$$

There are two special features added to this system of scopes by the schema notation. The first is that some declarations – those which call for the inclusion of a schema – do not mention explicitly the variable names being declared. If *Aleph* is the schema defined by

```
┌─ Aleph ─────────────────────────────
│  x, y : Z
│ ────────────────────────
│  x > y
└──────────────────────────────────────
```

then *Aleph* used as a declaration introduces the two variables x and y without naming them explicitly. The second special feature is that the components of a schema, although they are in some respects local to the schema's definition, cannot be renamed without affecting the meaning. For example, the schema *NewAleph* defined by

$$
\begin{array}{|l}
\hline
\rule{0pt}{1em}\textit{NewAleph} \underline{\hspace{6cm}}\\
\quad u, v : \mathbb{Z}\\
\hline
\quad u > v\\
\hline
\end{array}
$$

is different from *Aleph*, because it has different component names.

Nevertheless, the scope of the component names consists only of the predicate part of the schema, unless the schema is included in a declaration elsewhere, as explained above. Component names are also used in the notation $a.x$ for selecting a component x from a binding a, but, properly speaking, this is not a use of the *variable* x, but just of x as an *identifier*. Its meaning does not depend on x being in scope, because the information about which selectors are allowed is carried in the type of a.

Other kinds of name can appear in Z specifications besides variables. *Basic types* and *generic constants* respect the nesting of scopes. Basic type names may be global, or may be local to a generic definition, as described in Section 2.4. Generic constants are always global. Objects of each of these three kinds can be hidden by inner declarations of other objects with the same name, but it is not possible to have two different objects with the same name at the same level of nesting.

Schema names do not have any nesting of scope. Any name which is defined as a schema may only be used as such throughout the specification document. The first place in the specification where the name occurs must be its definition. A schema can have only one definition, and all uses of the name refer to this definition.

2.3.2 Schemas with global variables

So far, we have been considering schemas in isolation: the only variable names which have appeared in the predicate part have been the components of the schema (or if other names such as $+$ and $<$ have appeared, we have taken them for granted). This is not the whole story, however, because the use of names like $+$ and $<$ requires some explanation, and genuine global variables are an important feature of some specifications.

An example might be the specification of a counter whose value is always at most some limit yet to be determined. We might first

introduce, by an axiomatic description, a global variable *limit* to stand
for the maximum value to be taken by the counter:

$$\begin{array}{|l}
limit : \mathsf{N} \\
\hline
limit \leq 65535
\end{array}$$

Incidentally, the limit is itself restricted to be at most 65535. Now we
can define a schema to represent the state-space of the counter:

$$\begin{array}{|l}
\underline{COUNTER} \\
value : \mathsf{N} \\
\hline
value \leq limit
\end{array}$$

The predicate part of this schema mentions both the component *value*
and the global variable *limit*, constraining one to be no greater than
the other.

The global variable *limit* is part of the *global signature* of the specification, and the axiom *limit* $\leq$ 65535 contributes to a *global property*.
Together, these form an anonymous global schema, and all the named
schemas of the specification are seen a extensions of it. In a schema
definition, the component names of the schema are added to the global
signature to give the signature over which the predicate part is interpreted: in the schema *COUNTER*, this signature contains both *limit*
and *value*, and the predicate *value* < *limit* expresses a property over
this signature. The global property of the specification is incorpo-
rated in the property of every schema: in the example, the fact that
limit $\leq$ 65535 is part of the property of *COUNTER*, so we can conclude
that *value* $\leq$ 65535.

One way to understand a specification with global variables is to
imagine fixing on one situation for the global schema. This fixes the
values of the global variables, and the property of each schema then
places a restriction on the values of its components. As we vary the
global situation, the properties of the schemas will pick out different
ranges of possible values for the components; the specification describes
a family with one member for each situation satisfying the global property. If this family has more than one member, we say the specification
is *loose*. The *COUNTER* example is a loose specification, because the
predicate *limit* $\leq$ 65535 does not fix a single value for the global variable *limit*. The use of loose specifications for describing families of
abstract data types is described in Section 5.3.

Sometimes it happens that a component of a schema has the same
name as a global variable: in this case, the component hides the global

variable on the predicate part of the schema, which forms a 'hole' in the scope of the global variable. Occurrences of the name in the predicate part of the schema refer to the component, rather than the global variable.

2.4 Generic constructions

Many mathematical constructions are independent of the elements from which the construction starts: for example, we recognize sequences of numbers and sequences of characters as being the same kind of object, even though the elements they are built from – numbers and characters – are different, and we recognize concatenation of sequences as being the same operation whatever set the elements are drawn from. Similarly, we can often describe parts of computer systems independently of the particular data they operate on: a resource management module, for example, does the same kind of thing whether it is managing printers or disk drives.

The generic constructs of Z allow such families of concepts to be captured in a single definition. Z allows both generic constants, like the set of sequences over a particular set and the operation of concatenation, and generic schemas, like the state space of a resource manager. In the definition of these generic objects, the collection of basic types is locally extended with one or more *formal generic parameters*, which stand for the as-yet-unknown sets of elements on which the definition is based. Later, when the generic object is used, *actual generic parameters* are supplied; these determine the sets which the formal parameters take as their values.

The following generic schema *Pool* describes the state space of a generic resource manager. It has the set *RESOURCE* of resource units as a formal generic parameter, but assumes a set *USER* of user names from its context:

$$
\begin{array}{l}
\underline{\quad Pool[RESOURCE] \quad\rule{4cm}{0pt}} \\
\quad owner : RESOURCE \nrightarrow USER \\
\quad free : \mathbb{P}\ RESOURCE \\
\rule{7cm}{0.4pt} \\
\quad (\mathrm{dom}\ owner) \cup free = RESOURCE \\
\quad (\mathrm{dom}\ owner) \cap free = \varnothing \\
\end{array}
$$

The two components of this schema have types built upon both the basic types of the specification (e.g. *USER*) and the formal generic parameters (e.g. *RESOURCE*):

$owner : \mathbb{P}(RESOURCE \times USER)$; $free : \mathbb{P}\ RESOURCE$

The generic schema *Pool* might be instantiated to describe the state space of a particular resource manager, a pool of disks identified by numbers from 0 to 7:

$DiskPool \hat{=} Pool[0 \ .. \ 7]$

The actual generic parameter $0 \ .. \ 7$ has been supplied here; its type is $\mathbb{P}\ \mathsf{Z}$, so the signature of *DiskPool* is obtained by substituting Z for *RESOURCE* in the signature of *Pool*:

$owner : \mathbb{P}(\mathsf{Z} \times USER)$; $free : \mathbb{P}\ \mathsf{Z}$

More generally, if the type of the actual parameter is $\mathbb{P}\ t$, the signature of the instantiated schema is obtained by substituting t for the formal parameter. If there are several parameters, the substitutions of actual parameter types are performed simultaneously. The property part of the meaning of *DiskPool* includes the fact that *owner* is a partial function from $0 \ .. \ 7$ to *USER*, and that *free* is a subset of $0 \ .. \ 7$:

$owner \in 0 \ .. \ 7 \nrightarrow USER$

$free \in \mathbb{P}(0 \ .. \ 7)$

These constraints are implicit in the declaration of *owner* and *free*. The property of *DiskPool* also includes instantiated versions of the predicates from *Pool*:

$(\text{dom } owner) \cup free = 0 \ .. \ 7$

$(\text{dom } owner) \cap free = \varnothing$

More useful than generic schemas are generic constants: several dozen of them are defined in Chapter 4 to capture such concepts as relations, functions, sequences and the operations on them. An example is the function *first* for selecting the first element of an ordered pair:

$$
\begin{array}{l}
\underline{\overline{[X, Y]}} \\
\hline
first : X \times Y \to X \\
\hline
\forall x : X;\ y : Y \bullet first(x, y) = x \\
\end{array}
$$

This has two formal generic parameters X and Y, and defines a family of functions *first*. When one of these functions is used, we may supply the actual generic parameters explicitly, as in

$first[\mathsf{N}, \mathsf{N}]\ (3, 4) = 3$

or leave them implicit, as in the equivalent assertion

$first(3, 4) = 3$

The rules for determining implicit parameters from the context are given in Section 3.9.2.

A restriction must be obeyed in the definitions of generic constants for them to be mathematically sound: the definition must *uniquely determine* the value of the constant for each possible value of the formal parameters. For example, the following definition would not be allowed, because it does not specify which two elements of X are chosen as the values of *left* and *right* when there are more than two, nor which is chosen as *left* when there are exactly two. What's worse, no choice at all is possible when X is empty or has only one element.

$$
\begin{array}{|l}
\hline
[X] \\\\
\hline
left, right : X \\
\hline
left \neq right \\
\hline
\end{array}
$$

The requirement that generic definitions of constants uniquely determine the values of the constants places a proof obligation on the author of a specification, but it is one that is easily repaid when, for example, the constant is a function, and the predicate part of the definition contains an equation giving its value at each point of its domain.

2.5 Partially-defined expressions

The meaning of a mathematical expression can be explained by saying what value it takes in each situation: for example, the expression $x + y$ takes the value 5 in the situation where x is 2 and y is 3. An expression need not have a defined value in every situation: for example, the value of x div y is not defined in any situation where y is 0. We call such expressions *partially-defined*. The precise meaning of a partially-defined expression can be explained by saying in which situations its value is defined, and for each of these, what value the expression takes.

There are two constructions in Z which lead to partially-defined expressions. One is the application of a partial function such as the div operator, to arguments which may not be in its domain, and the other is the definite-description construct μ (see page 61).

Partially-defined expressions may appear in predicates of the form $E_1 = E_2$ or $E_1 \in E_2$, and it is necessary to say in what situations these predicates are true. As expected, whenever both E_1 and E_2 are defined, these two predicates express exactly the property that their values are equal, or respectively that the value of E_1 is a member of whatever set is the value of E_2. If one or both of E_1 and E_2 are undefined, then we say that the predicates $E_1 = E_2$ and $E_1 \in E_2$ are *undetermined*: we do not know whether they are true ar false. This does not mean that the predicates have some intermediate status in which they are 'neither true nor false', simply that we have chosen not to say whether they are true or not.

A common usage in Z specification is the predicate

$$x \in \operatorname{dom} f \wedge f(x) = y$$

As might be expected, this predicate asserts that x is in the domain of f and the value of f for argument x is y. We can reason as follows: if x is in the domain of f, then the conjunct $x \in \operatorname{dom} f$ will be true, so the whole predicate will be true exactly if the other conjunct, $f(x) = y$, is true also. If x is not in the domain of f, then $x \in \operatorname{dom} f$ is false, so the whole predicate is false whether $f(x) = y$ is true or not (in fact, it is undetermined). The predicate

$$x \in \operatorname{dom} f \Rightarrow f(x) = y$$

is true if *either* x is outside the domain of f, *or* the value of f at x is y. If the antecedent $x \in \operatorname{dom} f$ is false, the whole predicate is true, whatever the (undetermined) status of $f(x) = y$.

Partial functions may be defined by giving their domain and their value for each argument in the domain. A typical definition might look like this:

$$
\begin{array}{|l}
f : X \nrightarrow Y \\
\hline
\operatorname{dom} f = S \\
\forall x : S \bullet \\
\qquad f(x) = E
\end{array}
$$

Here, E is an expression which need only be defined in situations satisfying $x \in S$. By fixing the domain of f and its value at each point on the domain, this definition completely determines the partial function f.

CHAPTER THREE

The Z Language

The specification language described in this chapter is intended as a minimal language for specification in the Z style. For practical use, it needs to be augmented with the basic mathematical definitions in Chapter 4, and for some purposes it will need to be extended, perhaps with programming notations for expressing operation refinements, or with notations for expressing synchronization of concurrent processes. But the minimal language described here will be part of all these extensions, and any extension should be constructed on a mathematical foundation consistent with the one used here and presented in Chapter 2.

3.1 Syntactic conventions

The syntactic description of Z constructs given in this chapter is intended as a guide to the way the constructs look on paper: it treats each construct in isolation, and does not properly respect the relative binding powers of connectives and quantifiers, for example. A full grammar for Z is given in Chapter 6, and you should refer to this for the answers to any purely syntactic questions.

A few extensions to BNF are used to make the syntax descriptions more readable. The notation S;...;S stands for one or more instances of the syntactic class S, separated by semicolons; similarly, the notation S,...,S stands for one or more S's separated by commas. Slanted square brackets *[ ]* enclose items which are optional. Lists of items which may be empty are indicated by combining these two notations.

3.1.1 Words, decorations and identifiers

A word (Word) is the simplest kind of name in a Z specification: it is either a non-empty sequence of upper and lower case letters, digits, and underscores beginning with a letter, or a special symbol. Words are used as the names of schemas. An identifier (Ident) is a word followed by a decoration (Decoration), which is a possibly empty sequence of ', ? or ! characters:

Ident   ::=   Word Decoration

If a word is used in a specification as the name of a schema, it is called a *schema name* and is no longer available for use as in an ordinary identifier. Schemas are named with words rather than identifiers to allow for systematic decoration: if A is a schema and we write A', this means a copy of A in which all the component names have been decorated with '. When an identifier which already has a non-empty decoration is decorated, the two decorations are juxtaposed, with the new decoration on the right.

Some words are given the special status of prefix, infix, or postfix symbols. They belong to the syntactic classes In-Fun, Post-Fun, Pre-Rel, In-Rel, Pre-Gen, or In-Gen, depending on whether they are function (Fun), relation (Rel) or generic (Gen) symbols.

3.1.2 Prefix, infix and postfix symbols

The mathematical notation embodied in Z contains only a few basic forms of expression, but these are enough to express almost any mathematical property. For example, here is a predicate which expresses the fact that the sum of a and b is at least a:

$$(plus(a, b), a) \in geq$$

and here is a predicate which expresses the associativity of addition:

$$plus(plus(a, b), c) = plus(a, plus(b, c))$$

These predicates look quite unfamiliar, and any predicate much more complicated than these would become very difficult to read if expressed purely in these basic notations.

We can sugar the pill, however, by allowing infix symbols as abbreviations for the basic forms. If instead of $plus(x, y)$ we write $x + y$, and instead of $(x, y) \in geq$ we write $x \geq y$, then the two predicates take on a more familiar form:

$$a + b \geq a$$
$$(a + b) + c = a + (b + c)$$

This is possible because $+$ is an *infix function symbol* or *operator* in Z, and $\geq$ is an *infix relation symbol*.

Function symbols are of two kinds: infix function symbols, which appear between two arguments, and postfix function symbols, such as the transitive closure operators $^+$ and *, which follow a single argument. Expressions which use these symbols are abbreviations for the application of the function which is the value of the symbol, to an ordered pair of arguments or to a single argument respectively. There is no need for prefix function symbols, because ordinary symbols are taken as functions when they precede an argument.

Each infix function symbol has a priority, a number from 1 to 6, which determines the binding power of the symbol, with higher numbers indicating tighter binding. When function symbols of equal priority are used in the same expression, they associate to the left, so that $x + y + z$ means $(x + y) + z$.

There are two kinds of relation symbols: infix and prefix. Infix relation symbols have binary relations – sets of ordered pairs – as their values. A predicate may consist of two expressions separated by an infix relation symbol: the predicate is true if the values of the two expressions form an ordered pair in the relation. Prefix relation symbols simply have sets as their values. A predicate which consists of a prefix relation symbol followed by an expression is true if the value of the expression is an element of the set.

Infix relation symbols have no priority or association; instead, a sequence

$$E_1 \ R_1 \ E_2 \ R_2 \ \ldots \ R_{n-1} \ E_n$$

where the E_i are expressions and each R_i is '$=$' or '$\in$' or an infix relation symbol, is equivalent to the conjunction

$$E_1 \ R_1 \ E_2 \wedge E_2 \ R_2 \ E_3 \wedge \cdots \wedge E_{n-1} \ R_{n-1} \ E_n$$

Both function and relation symbols may be generic, and when they appear in expressions or predicates they are implicitly instantiated with actual generic parameters, as described in Section 3.9.2. In addition, there are infix generic symbols such as $\rightarrow$. These appear between two set-valued expressions which are actual generic parameters of the symbol. For example, in the expression $X \times Y \rightarrow Z$, the sub-expressions

$X \times Y$ and Z are generic parameters of the symbol $\rightarrow$. There are also unary prefix generic symbols such as $\mathbb{F}$, which precede a single set-valued expression. There is no priority among infix generic symbols. They bind less tightly than any function symbol, and they associate to the right, so that $A \rightarrow B \rightarrow C$ means $A \rightarrow (B \rightarrow C)$.

Sometimes it is necessary to name a symbol without applying it to arguments; this can be done by replacing the arguments with the special marker '$\_$'. So, for example, $\_ + \_$ is the name of a function which takes a pair of numbers and adds them; $\_ \geq \_$ is the name of an ordering relation on numbers; and $\_ \rightarrow \_$ is a generic symbol whose value is the total function space between its parameters. To avoid confusion, these names must be enclosed within parentheses whenever they appear as part of an expression. Using this notation, we can make explicit the expression for which each abbreviation stands:

$x + y$	is an abbreviation for	$(\_ + \_)(x, y)$
$x \geq y$	is an abbreviation for	$(x, y) \in (\_ \geq \_)$
$X \rightarrow Y$	is an abbreviation for	$(\_ \rightarrow \_)[X, Y]$
disjoint x	is an abbreviation for	$x \in (\text{disjoint } \_)$
$\mathbb{F} X$	is an abbreviation for	$(\mathbb{F} \_)[X]$
R^*	is an abbreviation for	$(\_^*)R$

The names are also used in declarations: for example,

$$\_ + \_ : \mathbb{Z} \times \mathbb{Z} \rightarrow \mathbb{Z}$$
$$\_ \geq \_ : \mathbb{Z} \leftrightarrow \mathbb{Z}$$

are the declarations of $+$ and $\geq$.

Some infix, prefix, and postfix symbols are standard; they are shown in the table below. Others may be introduced as they are needed, but each symbol should be used consistently throughout a document. Some specification tools work with a table of symbols which can be extended, but there is no standard way of doing this.

A few standard symbols do not fit in with the pattern described so far. The minus sign appears to be both an infix function symbol and an ordinary symbol, which may be applied as a function to a single number. The role played by the minus sign is decided by syntactic context, and its two roles are, in effect, two different symbols $(\_ - \_)$ and $(-)$, rather than two meanings overloaded on one symbol. Wherever possible, the minus sign is interpreted as an infix operator; the other interpretation can always be forced with parentheses. The notation $R(\!|S|\!)$ for the relational image of S through R is an abbreviation for the expression $(\_(\!|\_|\!))(R, S)$, in which the symbol $\_(\!|\_|\!)$ is applied to the pair

(R, S). The notation R^k for iteration of a relation is an abbreviation for the expression *iter k R*. Finally, the symbols $\upharpoonright$, $\setminus$, and $\,\fatsemi\,$ are used as operations in schema expressions as well as infix function symbols in ordinary expressions.

Standard symbols

Here are the standard symbols of the various kinds:

Infix function symbols (In-Fun)

> Priority 1: $\mapsto$
> Priority 2: $..$
> Priority 3: $+ \; - \; \cup \; \setminus \; ^\frown \; \uplus$
> Priority 4: $* \;\; \mathrm{div} \;\; \mathrm{mod} \; \cap \; \upharpoonright \; \fatsemi \; \circ$
> Priority 5: $\oplus$
> Priority 6: $\lhd \; \rhd \; \ntriangleleft \; \ntriangleright$

Postfix function symbols (Post-Fun)

> $\_^\sim \quad \_^* \quad \_^+$

Infix relation symbols (In-Rel)

> $\neq \; \notin \; \subseteq \; \subset \; < \; \leq \; \geq \; >$ in partition

Prefix relation symbols (Pre-Rel)

> disjoint

Infix generic symbols (In-Gen)

> $\leftrightarrow \;\; \nrightarrow \;\; \rightarrow \;\; \nrightarrowtail \;\; \rightarrowtail \;\; \nrightarrowtail \;\; \twoheadrightarrow \;\; \rightarrowtail \;\; \nrightarrow \;\; \twoheadrightarrow$

Prefix generic symbols (Pre-Gen)

> $\mathbb{P}_1 \;\; \mathrm{id} \;\; \mathbb{F} \;\; \mathbb{F}_1 \;\; \mathrm{seq} \;\; \mathrm{seq}_1 \;\; \mathrm{iseq} \;\; \mathrm{bag}$

3.1.3 Layout

In the formal text of a Z specification, spaces are generally not considered to be significant, except where they serve to separate one symbol from another. Line breaks are significant, because in an axiomatic description, vertical schema, or generic definition, line breaks may be used instead of semicolons in both the declaration part and the predicate part. Several newlines in succession are always regarded as equivalent to one, and newlines are ignored before and after infix function, relation and generic symbols, and before and after the following symbols:

$$; : , \mid \bullet == \; \hat{=} \; ::= \; = \; \in \; \wedge \; \vee \; \Rightarrow \; \Leftrightarrow \; \times \; \setminus \; \upharpoonright \; \fatsemi$$

In all these places, a semicolon would not be syntactically valid in any case.

3.2 Specifications

A Z specification document consists of interleaved passages of formal, mathematical text, and informal prose explanation. The formal text consists of a sequence of paragraphs which gradually introduce the schemas, global variables and basic types of the specification, each paragraph building on the ones which come before it. Except in the case of free type definitions (see Section 3.10), recursion is not allowed.

Each paragraph may define one or more names for schemas, basic types, global variables or global constants. It may use the names defined by preceding paragraphs, and the names it defines are available in the paragraphs which follow. This gradual building-up of the vocabulary of a specification is called the principle of *definition before use*. The scope of each global name extends from its definition to the end of the specification.

In presenting a formal specification, it is often convenient to show the paragraphs in an order different from the one they would need to have for the rule of definition before use to be obeyed. Some software tools may be able to perform analysis on specifications presented in this way, but there must always exist a possible order which obeys the rule. The account of the language in this manual assumes that the paragraphs of a specification are presented in this logical order.

There are several kinds of paragraph. Basic type definitions, axiomatic descriptions, constraints, schema definitions, and abbreviation definitions are described here; generic schema and constant definitions are described in Section 3.9; and free type definitions are described in Section 3.10.

3.2.1 Basic type definitions

Paragraph ::= [Ident, ... , Ident]

A basic type definition introduces one or more basic types. These names must not have a previous global declaration, and their scope extends from the definition to the end of the specification. The names become part of the global vocabulary of basic types.

An example of a basic type definition is the introduction of *NAME* and *DATE* in the birthday book example of Chapter 1:

[*NAME*, *DATE*]

3.2.2 Axiomatic descriptions

Paragraph ::= $\Big[$ $\begin{array}{|l} \text{Declaration} \\ \hline \text{Predicate; ...; Predicate} \end{array}$ $\Big]$

An axiomatic description introduces one or more global variables, and optionally specifies a constraint on their values. These variables must not have a previous global declaration, and their scope extends from their declaration to the end of the specification. The variables become part of the global signature of the specification. The predicates relate the values of the new variables to each other and to the values of previously-declared variables, and they become part of the global property. The italic square brackets *[...]* indicate that the dividing line and the predicate list below it are optional, so that

$\big|$ Declaration

is an acceptable form of axiomatic description. If the predicate part is absent, the default is the predicate *true*.

An example of an axiomatic description is the following definition of the function *square*:

$\begin{array}{|l} square : \mathbb{N} \to \mathbb{N} \\ \hline \forall n : \mathbb{N} \bullet \\ \quad square(n) = n * n \end{array}$

3.2.3 Constraints

Paragraph ::= Predicate

A predicate may appear on its own as a paragraph; it specifies a constraint on the values of previously-declared global variables. The effect is as if the constraint had been stated as part of the axiomatic description in which the variables were introduced.

An example of a constraint is the following predicate, which asserts that the variable n_disks has a value less than five:

$n\_disks < 5$

3.2.4 Schema definitions

Paragraph ::= $\Big[$

┌─Schema-Name────────────
│ Declaration
├────────────────
│ Predicate; ...; Predicate $\Big]$
└────────────────────

Paragraph ::= Schema-Name $\hat{=}$ Schema-Exp

These forms introduce a new schema name. The word heading the box or appearing on the left of the definition sign becomes associated with the schema which is the contents of the box or appears to the right of the definition sign. It must not have appeared previously in the specification, and from this point to the end of the specification it is a schema name. Again, if the predicate part in the vertical form is absent, the default is *true*.

The right-hand side of the horizontal form of schema definition is a schema expression, so new schemas may be defined by combining old ones with the operations of the schema calculus (see Section 3.8). The vertical form

┌─S────────────────────
│ $D_1; \ldots; D_m$
├────────────────
│ $P_1; \ldots; P_n$
└────────────────────

is equivalent to the horizontal form

$S \hat{=} [\, D_1; \ldots; D_m \mid P_1; \ldots; P_n \,]$

except that semicolons may be replaced by line breaks in the vertical form. The right-hand side of the horizontal form is a simple schema expression consisting of a schema text in square brackets.

Here is an example of a schema definition taken from the birthday book example:

BirthdayBook

$known : \mathbb{P} \; NAME$
$birthday : NAME \nrightarrow DATE$

$known = \operatorname{dom} birthday$

This definition may also be written in horizontal form:

$BirthdayBook \; \hat{=}$
    $[\, known : \mathbb{P} \; NAME; \; birthday : NAME \nrightarrow DATE \mid$
    $known = \operatorname{dom} birthday \,]$

The following definition of *RAddBirthday* uses a more complex schema expression on the right-hand side:

$RAddBirthday \; \hat{=} \; (AddBirthday \wedge Success) \vee AlreadyKnown$

3.2.5 Abbreviation definitions

Paragraph   ::=   Ident == Expression

An abbreviation definition introduces a new global constant. The identifier on the left becomes a global constant; its value is given by the expression on the right, and its type is the same as the type of the expression. The scope of the constant extends from here to the end of the specification. (In fact, this notation is a special case of the notation for defining generic constants: see Section 3.9.2.)

The following example of an abbreviation definition introduces the name *DATABASE* as an abbreviation for the set of functions from *ADDR* to *PAGE*:

$DATABASE == ADDR \rightarrow PAGE$

3.3 Schema references

When a schema name has been defined as described in Section 3.2.4, it can be used in a schema reference to refer to the schema. A schema reference can be used as a declaration, an expression, or a predicate, and it forms a basic element of schema expressions.

Schema-Ref   ::=   Schema-Name Decoration

A schema reference consists of a schema name followed by a decoration (which may be empty). It stands for a copy of the named schema in which the decoration has been systematically applied to all the components.

There is another form of schema reference with actual generic parameters used to instantiate a generic schema: see Section 3.9.1.

3.4 Declarations

Variables are introduced and associated with types by *declarations*. As explained above, a declaration may also require that the values of the variables satisfy a certain property, which we call the constraint of the declaration. There are two kinds of declaration in Z:

Basic-Decl   ::=   Ident, ... , Ident : Expression
       | Schema-Ref

The first kind introduces an explicitly-listed collection of variables. In the declaration

$$x_1, \ldots, x_n : E$$

the expression E must have a set type $\mathbb{P}\, t$ for some type t. The variables $x_1, \ldots, x_n$ are introduced with type t. The values of the variables are constrained to lie in the set E. For example, the declaration

$$p, q : 1 .. 10$$

introduces two variables p and q. The expression $1 .. 10$ has type $\mathbb{P}\, \mathbb{Z}$, for it is a set of integers. The type of p and q is therefore taken to be $\mathbb{Z}$: they are simply integers. This declaration constrains the values of p and q to lie between 1 and 10.

When a schema reference is used as a declaration, it introduces the components of the schema as variables, with the same types as they have in the schema, and constrains their values to satisfy its property. For example, if A is the schema

$$
\begin{array}{|l}
\hline
\;A\; \underline{\qquad\qquad\qquad\qquad\qquad\qquad\qquad\qquad} \\
\;x, y : \mathsf{Z} \\
\;\underline{\qquad\qquad\qquad\qquad} \\
\;x > y \\
\hline
\end{array}
$$

then the declaration A introduces the variables x and y, both of type Z, with the property that the value of x is greater than the value of y.

In every context where a single declaration is allowed, a sequence of declarations may also appear:

> Declaration   ::=   Basic-Decl; ...; Basic-Decl

This declaration introduces all the variables introduced by each of its constituent basic declarations, with the same types. The values of these variables are constrained to satisfy all the properties from the basic declarations. The same variable may be introduced by several of the basic declarations, provided it is given the same type in each of them: this rule allows schemas with common components to appear in the same declaration. The rule that types must match allows for the merging of common components.

The scope of the variables introduced by a declaration is determined by the context in which the declaration appears: they may be global to the whole of the succeeding specification, form the components of a schema, or be local to a predicate or expression. However, the scope never includes the declaration itself: variables may not be used on the right of a colon, nor as an actual generic parameter (see Section 3.9), in the declaration which introduces them.

3.4.1 Characteristic tuples

A set-comprehension expression has the form

> { Declaration | Predicate; ...; Predicate • Expression }

and its value is the set of values taken by the expression when the variables introduced by the declaration take all values which satisfy both the constraint of the declaration and the predicates (see page 60). The expression part may be omitted, and the default is then the *characteristic tuple* of the declaration. Characteristic tuples are also used in the definitions of λ and μ (see page 61).

To find the characteristic tuple of a declaration, first replace each multiple declaration

$$x_1, \ldots, x_n : E$$

by the following sequence of simple declarations:

$$x_1 : E; \ldots; x_n : E$$

Now form the list of *representatives* of the basic declarations:

- The representative of a simple declaration $x : E$ is the variable x; in the scope of the declaration, this has the type given to x by the declaration.

- The representative of a schema reference $A'[E_1, \ldots, E_n]$ is the θ-expression $\theta A'$ (see Section 3.6, page 64). In the scope of the declaration, this has a schema type whose components are the components of A, each with the type given to it by A.

If the list of representatives has exactly one member E, then the characteristic tuple is E; its type is simply the type of the only representative. Otherwise, the list of expressions contains $n \geq 2$ members $E_1, \ldots, E_n$, and the characteristic tuple is the tuple

$$(E_1, \ldots, E_n)$$

This has type $t_1 \times \cdots \times t_n$, where $t_1, \ldots, t_n$ are the types of the representatives $E_1, \ldots, E_n$ respectively.

Examples

- The characteristic tuple of the declaration $x, y : X; z : Z$ is (x, y, z). If X and Z are basic types, the type of this tuple is $X \times X \times Z$.

- The declaration A, where A is a schema, has characteristic tuple θA; its type is $\langle\!\langle x_1 : t_1; \ldots; x_n : t_n \rangle\!\rangle$, where $x_1, \ldots, x_n$ are the components of A and $t_1, \ldots, t_n$ respectively are their types in A.

- The characteristic tuple of the declaration $A; A'; x, y : X$ is the tuple $(\theta A, \theta A', x, y)$. Its type is $t \times t \times X \times X$, where t is the type of θA (and of $\theta A'$). This is so even if x is a component of A.

As the last example shows, a variable may be involved in more than one element of a characteristic tuple. If A is the schema defined by

$$A \mathrel{\widehat{=}} [\, x, y : \mathsf{N} \,]$$

then the set expression $\{\,A;\;\;x\;:\;\mathsf{N}\,\}$ is another way of writing the projection function $\lambda\,A\,\bullet\,x$. The characteristic tuple of the declaration $A;\;x:\mathsf{N}$ is $(\theta A,x)$, and both elements depend on x.

3.5 Schema texts

A schema text consists of a declaration and an optional list of predicates. Most Z constructs which introduce variables allow a schema text rather than simply a declaration, so that a relationship between the values of the variables can be described. Schema texts appear in vertical form in axiomatic descriptions and schema definitions, but they also have a horizontal form:

Schema-Text   ::=   Declaration $/|$ Predicate; ...; Predicate$/$

This form is used after the quantifiers $\forall$, $\exists$, and $\exists_1$, and in expressions formed with λ, μ, and $\{\,\}$ (set comprehension). A schema text in square brackets is the simplest kind of schema expression (see Section 3.8). If the optional list of predicates is absent, the default is the predicate *true*. The scope of the variables introduced by a schema text depends on the context in which it appears, but it always includes the predicate part of the schema text.

3.6 Expressions

The following pages contain concise descriptions of the basic forms of expression in Z:

$(\ldots)$, $\{\ldots\}$	Tuple and set display (p. 58)
$\mathbb{P}$, $\times$	Power set, Cartesian product (p. 59)
$\{\,\|\,\bullet\,\}$	Set comprehension (p. 60)
λ, μ	Lambda- and mu-expressions (p. 61)
Application	Function application (p. 62)
.	Selection (p. 63)
θ	Binding formation (p. 64)
Schema-Ref	Schema reference (p. 65)

These are the basic forms of expression, but as Section 3.1.2 explains, operator symbols allow the convenient abbreviation of certain common kinds of expression. For ease of reference, the rules for these are given explicitly on their own page:

Operators   Rules for operator symbols (p. 66)

Finally, some extra notations are introduced as part of the mathematical tool-kit in Chapter 4, and there is a page which summarizes these:

Displays   Notation for sequences and bags (p. 67)

Each page shows the syntax of the expressions, states any scope and type rules which must be obeyed, and describes the meaning. The meaning is fixed by saying in what situations an expression is defined, and when it is defined, what its value is (see Section 2.2 for an explanation of 'situations'). For expressions with optional parts, the defaults are stated.

An identifier forms the simplest kind of expression. It may be a local variable of the expression or an enclosing predicate, a component of a schema if the expression occurs in its definition, a global variable, or a global abbreviation or generic constant. Natural numbers may be expressed in decimal, and parentheses may be used for grouping in expressions:

Expression   ::=   Ident
             | Number
             | (Expression)

Name

(...)   –   Tuple
{...}   –   Set display

Syntax

Expression   ::=   (Expression, ..., Expression)
  | { [Expression, ..., Expression] }

To avoid ambiguity with parenthesized expressions, at least two expressions must appear in a tuple. There is no way to write a tuple containing fewer than two components.

To avoid ambiguity with set comprehension (see page 60), the list of expressions in a set display must not consist of a single schema-reference. A set display containing a single schema reference S can be written $\{(S)\}$.

Type rules

In the expression $(E_1, ..., E_n)$, if the arguments E_i have types t_i, then the expression itself has type $t_1 \times \cdots \times t_n$.

In the expression $\{E_1, ..., E_n\}$, each sub-expression E_i must have the same type t. The type of the expression is then $\mathbb{P}\, t$. See Section 3.9.2 for an explanation of what happens when $n = 0$.

Description

The expression $(x_1, ..., x_n)$ denotes an n-tuple whose components are $x_1, ..., x_n$.

The set $\{x_1, ..., x_n\}$ has as its only members the objects $x_1, ..., x_n$. Several of the x_i's may be equal, in which case the repetitions are ignored; since a set is characterized by which objects are members and which are not, the order in which the members are listed does not matter.

Laws

$$(x_1, ..., x_n) = (y_1, ..., y_n) \Leftrightarrow x_1 = y_1 \wedge \cdots \wedge x_n = y_n$$

$$y \in \{x_1, ..., x_n\} \Leftrightarrow y = x_1 \vee \cdots \vee y = x_n$$

Name

$\mathbb{P}$ –   Power set
$\times$ –   Cartesian product

Syntax

Expression ::= $\mathbb{P}$ Expression
          | Expression $\times \cdots \times$ Expression

Type rules

In the expression $\mathbb{P}\, E$, the argument E must have a set type $\mathbb{P}\, t$. The type of the expression is then $\mathbb{P}(\mathbb{P}\, t)$. For example, if E is a set of integers having type $\mathbb{P}\, \mathsf{Z}$, then $\mathbb{P}\, E$ has type $\mathbb{P}(\mathbb{P}\, \mathsf{Z})$ – it is a set of sets of integers. In the expression

$$E_1 \times \cdots \times E_n$$

each argument E_i must have a set type $\mathbb{P}\, t_i$. The type of the expression is then $\mathbb{P}(t_1 \times \cdots \times t_n)$. For example if E_1 has type $\mathbb{P}\, \mathsf{Z}$, and E_2 has type $\mathbb{P}\, CHAR$, then $E_1 \times E_2$ has type $\mathbb{P}(\mathsf{Z} \times CHAR)$ – it is a set of pairs, each containing an integer and a character.

Description

If S is a set, $\mathbb{P}\, S$ is the set of all subsets of S. If $S_1, \ldots, S_n$ are sets, then $S_1 \times \cdots \times S_n$ is the set of all n-tuples

$$(x_1, \ldots, x_n)$$

where $x_i \in S_i$ for each i with $1 \leq i \leq n$. Note that, for example, the sets $S \times T \times V$ and $S \times (T \times V)$ and $(S \times T) \times V$ are considered to be different.

Laws

$$S_1 \times \cdots \times S_n = \{\, x_1 : S_1;\ \ldots, x_n : S_n \bullet (x_1, \ldots, x_n)\,\}$$

Name

{ | • } – Set comprehension

Syntax

Expression   ::=   { Schema-Text $[$• Expression$]$ }

Defaults

If the expression part is omitted, the default is the characteristic tuple of the declaration appearing in the schema text part (see Section 3.4.1).

Scope rules

In the expression $\{ S \bullet E \}$, the schema text S introduces local variables; their scope includes the expression E.

Type rules

In the expression $\{ S \bullet E \}$, if the type of the sub-expression E is t, then the type of the expression is $\mathbb{P}\ t$.

Description

The members of the set $\{ S \bullet E \}$ are the values taken by the expression E when the variables introduced by S take all possible values which make the property of S true.

Laws

$$y \in \{ S \bullet E \} \Leftrightarrow \exists S \bullet y = E$$

provided y is not a variable of S.

Name

λ   –   Lambda-expression
μ   –   Mu-expression

Syntax

Expression   ::=   λ Schema-Text • Expression
             ::=   μ Schema-Text [• Expression]

Defaults

In a mu-expression, if the expression part is omitted, the default is the characteristic tuple of the declaration appearing in the schema text part (see Section 3.4.1).

Scope rules

In the expressions $\lambda S • E$ and $\mu S • E$, the schema text S introduces local variables; their scope includes the expression E.

Type rules

In the expression $\lambda S • E$, let t be the type of E, and let t' be the type of the characteristic tuple of the declaration appearing in S (see Section 3.4.1). The type of the whole expression is $\mathbb{P}(t' \times t)$.

In the expression $\mu S • E$, if the type of the sub-expression E is t, then the type of the expression is t also. If the expression E is omitted, the type of the expression is the type of the characteristic tuple of the declaration appearing in S.

Description

The expression $\lambda S • E$ denotes a function which takes arguments of a shape determined by S, and returns the result E. It is equivalent to the set comprehension $\{ S • (T, E) \}$, where T is the characteristic tuple of S.

The expression $\mu S • E$ is defined only if there is a unique way of giving values to the variables introduced by S which makes the property of S true; if this is so, then its value is the value of E when the variables introduced by S take these values.

Name

Application – Function application

Syntax

Expression ::= Expression Expression

Type rules

In the expression $E_1 E_2$, the sub-expression E_1 must have type $\mathbb{P}(t_1 \times t_2)$, and E_2 must have type t_1, for some types t_1 and t_2. The type of the whole expression is then t_2.

Description

The expression $E_1 E_2$ denotes the application of the function E_1 to the argument E_2. Strictly speaking, E_1 does not have to be a function, but for the expression to be defined, there must be a unique value y such that $(E_2, y) \in E_1$ (i.e. E_1 must be 'functional at E_2'), and the value of the expression is this y. Function applications are often written with parentheses round the argument, as in $f(x)$, but this is just a special case of the rule that allows brackets to be added around any expression. Application associates to the left, so $f\, x\, y$ means $(f\, x)\, y$: when f is applied to x, the result is a function, and this function is applied to y.

Laws

$$f(x) = (\mu\, y : Y \mid (x, y) \in f)$$

Name

. – Selection

Syntax

Expression   ::=   Expression . Ident

Type rules

In the expression $E.x$, the argument E must have a schema type $\langle y_1 : t_1; \ldots; y_n : t_n \rangle$, where the identifier x is identical with one of the component names y_i, for some i with $1 \leq i \leq n$. The type of the expression is the corresponding type t_i.

Description

This is the notation for selecting a component from a binding.

Laws

$$a.x = (\lambda\, S \bullet x)(a)$$

Name

θ – Binding formation

Syntax

Expression   ::= θ Schema-Name *[Decoration]*

Type rules

In the expression $\theta S'$, in which the symbol ' stands for an optional decoration, let the components of S be x_1, ..., x_n. The variables x_1', ..., x_n' must be in scope: let their types be t_1, ..., t_n. The type of the expression is the schema type

$$\langle x_1 : t_1; \ldots; x_n : t_n \rangle$$

Note that the components in this type have names without the decoration: this means that $\theta S'$ has the same type as θS.

Description

The value of the expression $\theta S'$ in any situation is a binding z with the schema type shown above; for each i with $1 \leq i \leq n$, the component $z.x_i$ is the value of the variable x_i' in that situation. If the optional decoration is absent, then it is the values of the undecorated variables x_i themselves which form the components $z.x_i$.

Note that the types of the components x_1, ..., x_n are taken from the current environment, and not from the schema S. There is no guarantee that their values satisfy the property of S, or even that the predicate $\theta S \in S$ is well-typed. If a new schema T is defined by

$$T \mathrel{\hat{=}} S'$$

then θT will have the type $\langle x_1' : t_1; \ldots; x_n' : t_n \rangle$, in which the component names are decorated; this is different from the type of $\theta S'$.

Laws

$$(\theta S').x_i = x_i'$$

$$\theta S' = \theta S \Leftrightarrow x_1' = x_1 \wedge \cdots \wedge x_n' = x_n$$

Name

Schema-Ref – Schema references as expressions

Syntax

Expression ::= Schema-Ref

where the decoration part of the schema reference is empty.

Type rules

The type of the schema reference S used as an expression is

$$\mathbb{P} \langle\!\langle x_1 : t_1; \ldots; x_n : t_n \rangle\!\rangle$$

where S has components $x_1, \ldots, x_n$ with types $t_1, \ldots, t_n$ respectively.

Description

A schema reference may be used as an expression: its value is the set of bindings in which the values of the components obey the property of the schema. The schema reference S used as an expression is equivalent to the set comprehension $\{ S \bullet \theta S \}$. The generic case is given as a law below.

Laws

$$S[E_1, \ldots, E_n] = \{ S[E_1, \ldots, E_n] \bullet \theta S \}$$

Name

Operators – Rules for infix and postfix function symbols

Syntax

Expression $::=$ Expression In-Fun Expression
$\quad\quad\quad\quad\quad |$ Expression Post-Fun

Type rules

In the expression $E_1 \, \omega \, E_2$, where ω is an infix function symbol, the type of ω must be $\mathbb{P}((t_1 \times t_2) \times t_3)$, and the types of the sub-expressions E_1 and E_2 must be t_1 and t_2 respectively, for some types t_1, t_2 and t_3. The type of the whole expression is t_3. Note that the type of ω is that of a function from $t_1 \times t_2$ to t_3.

In the expression $E \, \omega$, where ω is a postfix function symbol, the type of ω must be $\mathbb{P}(t_1 \times t_2)$, and the type of E must be t_1, for some types t_1 and t_2. The type of the whole expression is t_2. Note that the type of ω is that of a function from t_1 to t_2.

Description

The expression $E_1 \, \omega \, E_2$ is an abbreviation for $(\_ \, \omega \, \_)(E_1, E_2)$, the application of ω to the pair (E_1, E_2). According to the rules for function application, it is defined exactly when there is a unique y such that $((E_1, E_2), y) \in (\_ \, \omega \, \_)$, and its value is this y.

The expression $E \, \omega$ is an abbreviation for $(\_ \omega) \, E$, the application of ω to E. It is defined exactly when there is a unique y such that $(E, y) \in (\_ \omega)$, and its value is this y.

Laws

$$E_1 \, \omega \, E_2 = (\_ \, \omega \, \_)(E_1, E_2)$$

$$E \, \omega = (\_ \omega) \, E$$

Name

Displays – Notation for sequences and bags

Syntax

Expression   ::= $\langle$ [Expression, . . . , Expression] $\rangle$
       | [[[Expression, . . . , Expression]]]

Type rules

In the expression $\langle E_1, \ldots, E_n \rangle$, all the sub-expressions E_i must have the same type t. The type of the whole expression is $\mathbb{P}(\mathbb{Z} \times t)$; note that this is the type of a sequence of elements of t.

In the expression $[[E_1, \ldots, E_n]]$, all the sub-expressions E_i must have the same type t. The type of the whole expression is $\mathbb{P}(t \times \mathbb{Z})$; note that this is the type of a bag of elements of t.

Description

For a full description of these forms of expression, see the pages in Chapter 4 about sequences (page 118) and bags (page 127) respectively. The expressions are defined only if all the sub-expressions E_i are defined, and the value is then a sequence or bag made from these elements.

Laws

$$\langle x_1, x_2, \ldots, x_n \rangle = \{1 \mapsto x_1, 2 \mapsto x_2, \ldots, n \mapsto x_n\}$$

$$[[x_1, x_2, \ldots, x_n]] = \{x_1 \mapsto k_1, x_2 \mapsto k_2, \ldots, x_n \mapsto k_n\}$$

where, for each i, the number of times x_i appears in the list $x_1, x_2, \ldots, x_n$ is k_i.

3.7 Predicates

The following pages contain concise descriptions of the various forms
of predicate in Z:

$=, \in$	Equality, membership (p. 69)
$\neg, \wedge, \vee, \Rightarrow, \Leftrightarrow$	Propositional connectives (p. 70)
$\forall, \exists, \exists_1$	Quantifiers (p. 71)
Schema-Ref	Schema references (p. 72)

These are the basic forms of predicate, but as Section 3.1.2 explains,
relation symbols allow the convenient abbreviation of certain common
kinds of predicate. For ease of reference, the rules for these are given
explicitly:

Relations	Rules for relation symbols (p. 73)

Each page shows the syntax of the predicates, states any scope and type
rules which must be obeyed, and describes the meaning. The meaning
is fixed by saying what situations satisfy the predicate; see Section 2.2
for an explanation of 'situations'. For predicates with optional parts,
the defaults are stated.

Parentheses may be used for grouping in predicates, and the predicates *true* and *false* are the logical constants, satisfied by every situation and by no situation respectively:

Predicate	::=	(Predicate)
	|	*true*
	|	*false*

Name

= - Equality
∈ - Membership

Syntax

Predicate ::= Expression = Expression
| Expression ∈ Expression

Type rules

In the predicate $E_1 = E_2$, the expressions E_1 and E_2 must have the same type. In the predicate $E_1 \in E_2$, if E_1 has type t, then E_2 must have type $\mathbb{P}\ t$.

Description

The predicate $x = y$ is true if x and y are the same object. The predicate $x \in S$ is true if the object x is a member of the set S.

Laws

$x = x$

$x = y \Rightarrow y = x$

$x = y \wedge y = z \Rightarrow x = z$

If S and T are subsets of X,

$(\forall x : X \bullet x \in S \Leftrightarrow x \in T) \Leftrightarrow S = T$

Name

¬	–	Negation
∧	–	Conjunction
∨	–	Disjunction
⇒	–	Implication
⇔	–	Equivalence

Syntax

Predicate ::= ¬ Predicate
| Predicate ∧ Predicate
| Predicate ∨ Predicate
| Predicate ⇒ Predicate
| Predicate ⇔ Predicate

These connectives are shown in decreasing order of binding power; the connective ⇒ associates to the right, and the other binary ones associate to the left.

Description

These are the connectives of propositional logic; they allow complex predicates to be built from simpler ones in such a way that the truth or falsity of the compound in some situation depends only on the truth or falsity of the parts in the same situation. For example, the predicate $P_1 \land P_2$ is true in any situation if and only if both P_1 and P_2 are true in that situation. The following table lists the circumstances under which each kind of compound predicate is true:

$\neg\, P$	P is not true
$P_1 \land P_2$	Both P_1 and P_2 are true
$P_1 \lor P_2$	Either P_1 or P_2 or both are true
$P_1 \Rightarrow P_2$	Either P_1 is not true or P_2 is true or both
$P_1 \Leftrightarrow P_2$	Either P_1 and P_2 are both true, or they are both false.

Name

$\forall$ – Universal quantifier
$\exists$ – Existential quantifier
$\exists_1$ – Unique quantifier

Syntax

Predicate ::= $\forall$ Schema-Text • Predicate
| $\exists$ Schema-Text • Predicate
| $\exists_1$ Schema-Text • Predicate

The predicate governed by these quantifiers extends as far as possible to the right; the quantifiers bind less tightly than any of the propositional connectives.

Scope rules

In the predicates $\forall S • P$, $\exists S • P$, and $\exists_1 S • P$, the schema text S introduces local variables; their scope includes the predicate P.

Description

These are the quantifiers of predicate logic. The predicate $\forall S • P$ (pronounced 'For all S, P') is true if, whatever values are taken by the variables introduced by S which make the property of S true, the predicate P is true as well. The predicate $\exists S • P$ (pronounced 'There exists S such that P') is true if there is at least one way of giving values to the variables introduced by S so that both the property of S and the predicate P are true; the predicate $\exists_1 S • P$ (pronounced 'There is exactly one S such that P') is true if there is exactly one such way of giving values to the variables introduced by S.

Laws

$$(\forall D \mid P • Q) \Leftrightarrow (\forall D • P \Rightarrow Q)$$
$$(\exists D \mid P • Q) \Leftrightarrow (\exists D • P \wedge Q)$$
$$(\exists_1 D \mid P • Q) \Leftrightarrow (\exists_1 D • P \wedge Q)$$

$$(\exists S • P) \Leftrightarrow \neg (\forall S • \neg P)$$

$$(\exists_1 x : A • \ldots x \ldots) \Leftrightarrow$$
$$(\exists x : A • \ldots x \ldots \wedge (\forall y : A \mid \ldots y \ldots • y = x))$$

Name

Schema-Ref   –   Schema references as predicates

Syntax

Predicate   ::=   Schema-Ref
          | pre Schema-Ref

In the form 'pre Schema-Ref', the decoration part of the schema reference must be empty.

Scope and type rules

In the predicate S', where S is a schema name, all the components of the decorated schema S' must be in scope, and they must have the same types as in the signature of the schema.

In the predicate 'pre S', where S is a schema, all the components of the schema S except those decorated with a single ' or ! must be in scope, and must have the same type as in the signature of the schema.

Description

A schema reference S' may be used as a predicate: it is true in exactly those situations which, when restricted to the signature of the schema, satisfy its property. It is effectively equivalent to the predicate $\theta S' \in S$, where S as an expression means $\{\, S \bullet \theta S \,\}$. The generic case is given as a law below.

The predicate 'pre S' is used when S is a schema describing an operation under the conventions explained in Chapter 5. It is equivalent to the predicate $PreS$, where $PreS$ is a schema defined by

$PreS \mathrel{\hat=} \text{pre } S$

(compare page 77). If *State* describes the state space of the operation S and its output is $y! : Y$, the predicate 'pre S' is also equivalent to $\exists \, State';\ y! : Y \bullet S$.

Laws

$$S'[E_1, \ldots, E_n] \Leftrightarrow \theta S' \in \{\, S[E_1, \ldots, E_n] \bullet \theta S \,\}$$

Name

Relations – Rules for relation symbols

Syntax

Predicate   ::=   **Expression In-Rel Expression ...**
            | **Pre-Rel Expression**

Type rules

In the predicate $E_1 \ R \ E_2$, where R is an infix relation symbol, R must have type $\mathbb{P}(t_1 \times t_2)$, and E_1 and E_2 must have types t_1 and t_2 respectively, for some types t_1 and t_2.

In the predicate $R \ E$, where R is a prefix relation symbol, R must have type $\mathbb{P} \ t$, and E must have type t, for some type t.

Description

As explained in Section 3.1.2, the chain of relationships

$E_1 \ R_1 \ E_2 \ R_2 \ \ldots \ R_{n-1} \ E_n$

is equivalent to the conjunction of the individual relationships:

$E_1 \ R_1 \ E_2 \wedge E_2 \ R_2 \ E_3 \wedge \cdots \wedge E_{n-1} \ R_{n-1} \ E_n$

The equality and membership signs $=$ and $\in$ may also appear in such a chain: they can be used like built-in relation symbols. This rule explains arbitrary chains of relations in terms of simple relationships $E_1 \ R \ E_2$, for which the type rule is given above. Such a relationship is a shorthand for $(E_1, E_2) \in (\_ \ R \ \_)$, and it is satisfied exactly if whatever set is the value of R contains the ordered pair (E_1, E_2).

The predicate $R \ E$, where R is a prefix relation symbol, is a shorthand for $E \in (R \ \_)$; it is satisfied exactly if the value of E is a member of whatever set is the value of R.

3.8 Schema expressions

The following pages describe the syntax of the various kinds of schema expression:

$\neg, \wedge, \vee, \Rightarrow, \Leftrightarrow$ Logical schema operations (p. 75)

$\forall, \exists, \exists_1, \backslash, \upharpoonright$ Hiding operations (p. 76)

pre, $\,_9^o$ Special-purpose operations (p. 77)

The meanings of these forms of expression are given in Section 2.2.3.

The simplest kinds of schema expression are schema references (see Section 3.3) and schema texts (see Section 3.5). Parentheses may be used for grouping in schema expressions.

```
Schema-Exp   ::=   Schema-Ref
             |     [ Schema-Text ]
             |     (Schema-Exp)
```

Name

¬ – Schema negation
∧ – Schema conjunction
∨ – Schema disjunction
⇒ – Schema implication
⇔ – Schema equivalence

Syntax

Schema-Exp   ::=   ¬ Schema-Exp
              | Schema-Exp ∧ Schema-Exp
              | Schema-Exp ∨ Schema-Exp
              | Schema-Exp ⇒ Schema-Exp
              | Schema-Exp ⇔ Schema-Exp

Description

These are the logical operations on schemas which were introduced
in Section 2.2.3. The negation ¬ S of a schema S has the same
signature as S, but its property is true in just those situations
where the property of S is not true.

For one of the binary operations to be defined, its two arguments
must have type compatible signatures. The signatures are joined
to form the signature of the result, and the truth of its property in
a situation depends on the truth of the properties of the arguments
in the restrictions of that situation. For example, the property
of $S \vee T$ is true in a situation exactly if either or both of the
restrictions of the situation to the signatures of S and T satisfy
their respective properties. The other operations follow the rules
for propositional connectives (see page 70).

Name

∀   –   Universal schema quantifier
∃   –   Existential schema quantifier
$\exists_1$ –   Unique schema quantifier
\   –   Schema hiding
↾   –   Schema projection

Syntax

Schema-Exp   ::=   ∀ Schema-Text • Schema-Exp
         | ∃ Schema-Text • Schema-Exp
         | $\exists_1$ Schema-Text • Schema-Exp
         | Schema-Exp \ (Ident, . . . , Ident)
         | Schema-Exp ↾ Schema-Exp

Description

These operations are grouped together because they all hide some of the components of their argument schemas: the three quantifiers hide the variables introduced by the schema text immediately following the quantifier, and the hiding operation \ hides the identifiers explicitly listed as its second argument. The schema projection operator ↾ hides all the components of its first argument except the ones which are also components of its second argument. For the definitions of these operations, see Section 2.2.3.

Name

pre   –   Pre-condition
⨟   –   Sequential composition

Syntax

Schema-Exp   ::=   pre Schema-Exp
          | Schema-Exp ⨟ Schema-Exp

Description

These two schema operations are useful in describing sequential systems. They depend on the conventions for decorating inputs and outputs and the states before and after an operation: for details, see Chapter 5.

If S is a schema, and $x'_1, \ldots, x'_m$ are the components of S ending in $'$, and $y_1!, \ldots, y_n!$ are the components ending in !, then the schema 'pre S' is the result of hiding these variables of S:

$$S \setminus (x'_1, \ldots, x'_m, y_1!, \ldots, y_n!)$$

It contains only the components of S corresponding to the state before the operation and its input.

For the composition $S \mathbin{⨟} T$ to be defined, the primed components of S must match the undecorated components of T, in the sense that S has a variable x' if and only if T has a variable x, and their types are the same. Also, the types of any input or output components they share must be the same. The schema $S \mathbin{⨟} T$ has all the undecorated components of S and all the primed components of T, together with all their input and output components. Let $State$ be a schema containing just the undecorated components of T, so that $State'$ contains exactly the primed components of T. The schema $S \mathbin{⨟} T$ is defined to be

$\exists\, State'' \bullet$
    $(\exists\, State' \bullet [\, S \mid \theta State' = \theta State'' \,]) \land$
    $(\exists\, State \;\bullet [\, T \mid \theta State = \theta State'' \,])$

In this definition, $State''$ is the hidden state in which S terminates and T starts.

3.9 Generics

The generic constructs of Z allow generic schemas and constants to be defined and applied. The ideas behind generics are explained in Section 2.4. This section contains a description of the syntax of the paragraphs which define generic schemas and constants, and the rules for using them. The type rules explained in Section 3.9.2 are also used to infer the types of empty set, sequence, and bag displays (see Section 3.6).

3.9.1 Generic schemas

Generic schemas have definitions similar to those of ordinary schemas, but with generic parameters:

$$\text{Paragraph} \quad ::= \quad \left[\begin{array}{l} \underline{\text{Schema-Name}[\text{Ident}, \ldots, \text{Ident}]} \\ \text{Declaration} \\ \hline \text{Predicate}; \ \ldots; \ \text{Predicate} \end{array} \right]$$

$$\text{Paragraph} \quad ::= \quad \text{Schema-Name}[\text{Ident}, \ldots, \text{Ident}] \;\hat{=}\; \text{Schema-Exp}$$

In the body or the right-hand side of the definition, the collection of basic types is locally extended with the formal generic parameters. As for ordinary schemas, the name must not have appeared before in the specification, and it becomes a schema name. Each use of the name, except in a θ-expression (see page 64), must be supplied with actual generic parameters:

$$\text{Schema-Ref} \quad ::= \\ \qquad \text{Schema-Name Decoration } [\text{Expression}, \ldots, \text{Expression}]$$

The signature of the resulting schema is obtained by applying the decoration to the variables of the generic schema and substituting the types of the actual parameters for the formal parameters. The property of the result is augmented with the constraint that the formal parameters take as their values whatever sets are the values of the actual parameters. For an explanation and an example of this, see Section 2.4.

3.9.2 Generic constants

Generic constants can be defined with a paragraph which looks like an axiomatic description but has a double bar on top with formal generic parameters:

$$
\text{Paragraph} \quad ::= \quad \left[\begin{array}{l} \rule[0.5ex]{1.5em}{0.4pt}\!\!\!\!\!/\,[\text{Ident}, \ldots, \text{Ident}]\,/\rule[0.5ex]{4em}{0.4pt} \\[2pt] \text{Declaration} \\[2pt] \hline \\[-8pt] \text{Predicate}; \ldots; \text{Predicate} \quad / \end{array} \right.
$$

The formal generic parameters are local to the definition, and each variable introduced by the declaration becomes a global generic constant. These identifiers must not previously have been defined as global variables or generic constants, and their scope extends from here to the end of the specification. The predicates must determine the values of the constants uniquely for each value of the formal parameters.

Generic constants may also be introduced by an abbreviation definition in which the left-hand side has generic parameters:

Paragraph ::= Def-Lhs == Expression

Def-Lhs ::= Ident $/$[Ident, . . . , Ident]$/$
     | Ident In-Gen Ident
     | Pre-Gen Ident

This is a generalization of the simple abbreviation facility described in Section 3.2.5. The left-hand side may be a pattern containing a prefix or infix generic symbol: an example is the definition

$$X \leftrightarrow Y == \mathbb{P}(X \times Y)$$

of the relation sign ($\_ \leftrightarrow \_$). The formal generic parameters are local to right-hand side, and the left-hand side becomes a global generic constant. It must not previously have been defined as a global variable or generic constant, and its scope extends from here to the end of the specification.

When a generic constant is used, the actual generic parameters may be supplied explicitly or left implicit.

Expression ::= Ident $/$[Expression, . . . , Expression]$/$

The form $E_1 \, \omega \, E_2$, where ω is an infix generic symbol, is an abbreviation for $(\_\omega\_)[E_1, E_2]$, and the form $\omega \, E$, where ω is a prefix generic symbol, is an abbreviation for $(\omega\_)[E]$. If actual parameters are left implicit, they are inferred from the typing information in the expression: they are chosen to be whatever types make the expression obey the type rules. If there are no such types, the expression is wrong; likewise if there are several ways of filling in types as the actual parameters, the expression is wrong, and more information needs to be made explicit. For example, consider the generic function *first* defined by

$$\begin{array}{|l}
\hline
\llcorner[X, Y]\underline{\hspace{4cm}}\\
\quad first : X \times Y \rightarrow X\\
\hline
\quad \forall x : X;\ y : Y \bullet first(x, y) = x\\
\hline
\end{array}$$

In the expression $first(3, 4)$, the generic constant *first* must have type

$$\mathbb{P}((\alpha \times \beta) \times \alpha)$$

where α and β are the types filled in for the two generic parameters X and Y. Its argument $(3, 4)$ has type $\mathsf{Z} \times \mathsf{Z}$, so α and β must both be Z, and the type of the whole expression $first(3, 4)$ is Z:

$$first(3, 4) = first[\mathsf{Z}, \mathsf{Z}](3, 4)$$

One kind of error is illustrated by the expression $first\ \{3, 4\}$. The function *first* must again have a type matching the pattern $\mathbb{P}((\alpha \times \beta) \times \alpha)$. This time, however, the type of the argument $\{3, 4\}$ is $\mathbb{P}\ \mathsf{Z}$, and this does not match $\alpha \times \beta$: there is no choice of the generic parameters which makes the expression obey the type rules, and it is wrong.

The expression $first(3, \varnothing)$ illustrates the other kind of error. Here the second component of the argument, $\varnothing$, is itself generic. It is defined by

$$\begin{array}{|l}
\hline
\llcorner[X]\underline{\hspace{4cm}}\\
\quad \varnothing : \mathbb{P}\ X\\
\hline
\quad \varnothing = \{\ x : X \mid false\ \}\\
\hline
\end{array}$$

and its type is $\mathbb{P}\ \gamma$, where γ is the type filled in for the generic parameter X. So the argument $(3, \varnothing)$ has type $(\mathsf{Z} \times \mathbb{P}\ \gamma)$, and matching this with $\alpha \times \beta$ gives $\alpha = \mathsf{Z}$ and $\beta = \mathbb{P}\ \gamma$. We are tempted to deduce that Z is the type of the whole expression, but this is not so, since the type γ is undetermined: there is more than one way of filling in the types. In this example, the indefiniteness seems rather benign, since the value of the expression $first(3, \varnothing)$ does not depend on the type chosen as γ; but other cases are not so simple, and this is the reason for the general rule. The error of leaving types undetermined can usually be avoided by supplying one or actual parameters explicitly: as in the legal expression $first(3, \emptyset[Z])$.

The method used in these examples can be used generally for inferring actual generic parameters which have been left implicit: the unknown types are represented by place-markers like those written with Greek letters above. When two types are required to be the same by the type rules, the two types (possibly containing place-markers) are matched with each other by *unification*, and an expression is correctly typed exactly if the type rules give enough information to eliminate all the unknowns. The same method allows type checking of the empty set $\{\}$, the empty sequence $\langle\rangle$, and the empty bag $[\![]\!]$: these can have any types $\mathbb{P}\,\alpha$, $\mathbb{P}(Z \times \beta)$, and $\mathbb{P}(\gamma \times Z)$ respectively, where α, β, and γ are unknowns.

3.10 Free types

The notation for free type definitions adds nothing to the power of the Z language, but it makes it easier to describe recursive structures such as lists and trees. The syntax of a free type definition is as follows:

$$\text{Paragraph} \quad ::= \quad \text{Ident} ::= \text{Branch} \mid \ldots \mid \text{Branch}$$

$$\text{Branch} \quad ::= \quad \text{Ident} \,[\, \langle\!\langle \text{Expression} \rangle\!\rangle \,]$$

(In the first of these syntax rules, the second occurrence of the symbol '::=' stands for exactly that symbol.) The meaning of this construct is given here by showing how to translate free type definitions into the other Z constructs. In the translation, we shall use for convenience some of the notation introduced in Chapter 4 on 'the mathematical tool-kit'. A free type definition

$$T ::= c_1 \mid \ldots \mid c_m \mid d_1 \langle\!\langle E_1[T] \rangle\!\rangle \mid \ldots \mid d_n \langle\!\langle E_n[T] \rangle\!\rangle$$

introduces a new basic type T, and $m + n$ new variables $c_1, \ldots, c_m$ and $d_1, \ldots, d_n$, declared as if by

$[T]$

$\begin{array}{|l}
\hline
\quad c_1, \ldots, c_m : T \\
\quad d_1 : E_1[T] \rightarrowtail T \\
\quad \ldots \\
\quad d_n : E_n[T] \rightarrowtail T \\
\hline
\quad \ldots \\
\end{array}$

The c_i's are constants of type T, and the d_j's, called the *constructors*, are injections from the sets $E_j[T]$ to T. What makes things interesting is that the expressions $E_j[T]$ may contain occurrences of T; I have used the notation $E_j[T]$ to make explicit the possibility that these expressions depend on T.

Although the free type definition itself appears to be circular, since the name T being defined appears on the right as well as on the left, this translation removes the circularity, since T is introduced as a basic type *before* the d_i's are declared.

There are two axioms constraining the constants and constructors. First, all the constants are distinct, and the constructors have disjoint ranges which do not contain any of the constants:

$$\text{disjoint}\ \langle\{c_1\},\ldots,\{c_m\},\operatorname{ran} d_1,\ldots,\operatorname{ran} d_n\rangle$$

Second, the smallest subset of T which contains all the constants and is *closed under the constructors* is T itself. In the following axiom, $E_j[W]$ is the expression which results from replacing all free occurrences of T in $E_j[T]$ by W, a name appearing nowhere else in the specification. The axiom is an *induction principle* for the free type:

$$\forall W : \mathbb{P}\, T \bullet$$
$$\{c_1,\ldots,c_m\} \cup d_1(\!|E_1[W]|\!) \cup \cdots \cup d_n(\!|E_n[W]|\!) \subseteq W$$
$$\Rightarrow T \subseteq W$$

One consequence of this induction principle is that the constants and constructors together exhaust the whole of T, so that

$$\langle\{c_1\},\ldots,\{c_m\},\operatorname{ran} d_1,\ldots,\operatorname{ran} d_n\rangle\ \text{partition}\ T$$

The induction principle also justifies the method of proof by induction described below.

3.10.1 Example: binary trees

The details of this axiomatization are a little difficult to understand all at once, but a small example will help to make things clear. We can describe the set of binary trees labelled with natural numbers by saying that the constant *tip* is a tree (the empty one), and that if n is a number and t_1 and t_2 are trees, then $fork(n, t_1, t_2)$ is a tree:

$$TREE ::= tip \mid fork\langle\!\langle \mathbb{N} \times TREE \times TREE \rangle\!\rangle$$

This free type definition is equivalent to the following axiomatic description:

[*TREE*]

> *tip* : *TREE*
> *fork* : N × *TREE* × *TREE* ↣ *TREE*
> ___
> disjoint ⟨{*tip*}, ran *fork*⟩
> ∀ *W* : P *TREE* •
>   {*tip*} ∪ *fork*(|N × *W* × *W*|) ⊆ *W*
>   ⇒ *TREE* ⊆ *W*

Since *fork* is an injection, putting together different trees, or the same trees with a different label, gives different results. The range of *fork* is disjoint from the set {*tip*}, that is

$$tip \notin \operatorname{ran} fork$$

so *tip* cannot result from putting two trees together with *fork*.

The induction principle justifies proofs by structural induction on trees, which are analogous to the proofs by induction on natural numbers, finite sets, and sequences described in Chapter 4. Suppose we want to prove that a predicate $P(t)$ is true of all trees t. The induction principle says that it is enough to prove the following two facts:

(a1) $P(tip)$ holds.

(a2) If $P(t_1)$ and $P(t_2)$ hold, so does $P(fork(n, t_1, t_2))$:

> ∀ *n* : N; t_1, t_2 : *TREE* •
> $P(t_1) \land P(t_2) \Rightarrow P(fork(n, t_1, t_2))$

If these facts hold, the induction principle lets us derive ∀ *t* : *TREE* • $P(t)$. Let *W* be the set of trees satisfying *P*: that is,

$$W = \{\, t : TREE \mid P(t) \,\}$$

Fact (a1) says that $tip \in W$, and fact (a2) says that $fork$(|N × *W* × *W*|) ⊆ *W*, so by the induction principle, *TREE* ⊆ *W*. This means that ∀ *t* : *TREE* • $t \in W$, or equivalently, that ∀ *t* : *TREE* • $P(t)$.

3.10.2 Consistency

There is a snag with the notation for defining free types, and that is the possibility that the definition will be inconsistent: that there will be no sets and functions which satisfy the axioms given above. The classic example of an inconsistent free type definition is that of a type containing both natural numbers as atoms, and all the functions from the type to itself:

$$T ::= atom\langle\!\langle \mathsf{N} \rangle\!\rangle \mid fun\langle\!\langle T \to T \rangle\!\rangle$$

Briefly, no such set T can exist, because however large T is, there are many more functions from T to T than there are members of T.

A sufficient condition for a free type definition

$$T ::= c_1 \mid \ldots \mid c_m \mid d_1\langle\!\langle E_1[T] \rangle\!\rangle \mid \ldots \mid d_n\langle\!\langle E_n[T] \rangle\!\rangle$$

to be consistent is that all the constructions $E_1[T], \ldots, E_n[T]$ which appear on the right-hand side are *finitary*, in a sense explained below. Examples of finitary constructions include Cartesian products $X \times Y$, finite sets $\mathbb{F}\, X$, finite functions $X \nrightarrow Y$, and finite sequences $\operatorname{seq} X$, as well as set constants not containing the type T being defined. Any composition of finitary constructions is also finitary. Any construction on T which involves objects containing infinitely many elements of T will not be finitary – for example, the power-set construction $\mathbb{P}\, T$ and infinite sequences $\mathsf{N} \to T$ are not finitary.

The examples just given provide enough finitary constructions for most practical purposes; but for completeness, here is a precise definition of the concept of finitary construction. Informally speaking, a construction $E[T]$ is finitary if each of its elements can be obtained by 'putting together' finitely many elements of T.

We say that $E[T]$ is *monotonic* if whenever $T \subseteq V$, then also $E[T] \subseteq E[V]$. This is a reasonable property to require of constructions, because a construction should not produce less when we give it more material to work on. Now let a chain on a set X be an infinite sequence of subsets of X with each member a subset of the next. In Z:

$$CHAIN[X] == \{\, S : \mathsf{N} \to \mathbb{P}\, X \mid (\forall i : \mathsf{N} \bullet S(i) \subseteq S(i+1)) \,\}$$

The limit of a chain is just the union of all its members:

$$
\begin{array}{l}
\rule{0pt}{0pt}[X]\\
\hline
\lim : CHAIN[X] \to \mathbb{P}\, X \\
\hline
\forall S : CHAIN[X] \bullet \\
\quad \lim S = \bigcup \{\, i : \mathsf{N} \bullet S(i) \,\}
\end{array}
$$

If S is a chain, and $E[T]$ is a monotonic construction, then the function

$$\lambda\, i : \mathsf{N} \bullet E[S(i)]$$

will also be a chain. We say that $E[T]$ is finitary if it is monotonic, and the limit of this chain is always equal to the result of applying E to $\lim S$:

$$\forall S : CHAIN[X] \bullet$$
$$\lim(\lambda\, i : \mathsf{N} \bullet E[S(i)]) = E[\lim S]$$

This property must hold whatever set is taken as the generic parameter X: it should be proved as a theorem generic in X. In mathematical terminology, $E[T]$ is finitary if it is 'continuous with respect to $\subseteq$'.

If each element of $E[\lim S]$ results from 'putting together' finitely many elements of T, then for each element x there will be some stage $S(n)$ in the chain by which all the constituents of x have appeared. This means that x will be in $E[S(n)]$, and so in the limit on the left hand side.

CHAPTER FOUR

The Mathematical Tool-kit

An important part of the Z method is a standard library or tool-kit of mathematical definitions. This tool-kit allows many structures in information systems to be described very compactly, and because the data types it contains are oriented towards mathematical simplicity rather than computer implementation, reasoning about properties of the systems is made easier. This chapter consists almost entirely of independent manual pages, each introducing an operation or group of related operations from the tool-kit. Each page includes laws which relate its operations to each other and to the operations defined on preceding pages. These laws are stated without explicitly declaring the variables they contain; their types should be clear from the context. A number of pages consist entirely of laws of a certain kind: for example, the induction principles for natural numbers and for sequences are summarized on their own pages.

The tool-kit begins with the basic operations of set algebra (Section 4.1). Many of these operations have a strong connection with the subset ordering $\subseteq$, and the laws relating them are listed on a separate page.

$\neq, \notin$	Inequality, non-membership (p. 89)
$\varnothing, \subseteq, \subset, \mathbb{P}_1$	Empty set, subsets, non-empty sets (p. 90)
$\cup, \cap, \setminus$	Set algebra (p. 91)
$\bigcup, \bigcap$	Generalized union and intersection (p. 92)
first, *second*	Projection functions for ordered pairs (p. 93)
$\bullet$	Order properties of set operations (p. 94)

Next, the idea of a relation as a set of ordered pairs is introduced, together with various operations on relations (Section 4.2). Again, the subset ordering plays a special part, in that many of the operations are monotonic with respect to it: these laws are shown on their own page.

In Section 4.3, functions are introduced as a special kind of relation. Injections, surjections and bijections are introduced as special kinds of function. Because functions are really relations, the operations on relations may be used on functions too. Extra laws about this usage are listed on a separate page.

Natural numbers are introduced in Section 4.4, together with the ideas of iteration of a relation and of finite sets and functions. Induction is an important proof method for natural numbers, and it is given its own page.

Sequences are introduced as functions whose domains are certain segments of the natural numbers (Section 4.5). There are several important operations on sequences, and they inherit the operations on relations; some extra laws about these are listed on a separate page.

There are specialized induction principles for sequences, and these too have their own page.

Bags are like sets, except that it matters how many times a bag contains each of its elements. The notion of bag and some operations on bags are defined in Section 4.6.

This chapter may be used as a formal specification of the tool-kit by extracting just the 'definition' parts. The principle of definition before use has been observed in all but two cases: the relation symbol $\leftrightarrow$ and the function symbol $\rightarrow$. For completeness, their definitions are given here:

$$X \leftrightarrow Y == \mathbb{P}(X \times Y)$$
$$X \rightarrow Y == \{\, f : X \leftrightarrow Y \mid \forall x : X \bullet \exists_1 y : Y \bullet (x,y) \in f \,\}$$

4.1 Sets

Name

$\neq$ – Inequality
$\notin$ – Non-membership

Definition

$$\begin{array}{|l}
\hline
\llcorner [X] \underline{} \\
\quad \_ \neq \_ : X \leftrightarrow X \\
\quad \_ \notin \_ : X \leftrightarrow \mathbb{P}\, X \\
\hline
\quad \forall x, y : X \bullet x \neq y \Leftrightarrow \neg\,(x = y) \\
\quad \forall x : X;\ S : \mathbb{P}\, X \bullet x \notin S \Leftrightarrow \neg\,(x \in S) \\
\hline
\end{array}$$

Description

The relations $\neq$ and $\notin$ are the complements of the equality and membership relations expressed by $=$ and $\in$ respectively.

Laws

$$x \neq y \Rightarrow y \neq x$$

Name

$\emptyset$ –   Empty set
$\subseteq$ –   Subset relation
$\subset$ –   Proper subset relation
$\mathbb{P}_1$ –   Non-empty subsets

Definition

$\emptyset[X] == \{\, x : X \mid \textit{false} \,\}$

$$
\begin{array}{|l}
\hline
[X]\,\rule{4cm}{0.4pt} \\
\hline
\_ \subseteq \_,\_ \subset \_ : \mathbb{P}\,X \leftrightarrow \mathbb{P}\,X \\
\hline
\forall S, T : \mathbb{P}\,X \bullet \\
\quad (S \subseteq T \Leftrightarrow (\forall x : X \bullet x \in S \Rightarrow x \in T)) \wedge \\
\quad (S \subset T \Leftrightarrow S \subseteq T \wedge S \neq T) \\
\hline
\end{array}
$$

$\mathbb{P}_1 X == \{\, S : \mathbb{P}\,X \mid S \neq \emptyset \,\}$

Description

$\emptyset$ is the empty set. It has no members.

A set S is a *subset* of a set T ($S \subseteq T$) if every member of S is also a member of T. We say S is a *proper subset* of T ($S \subset T$) if in addition S is different from T.

For any set X, $\mathbb{P}_1 X$ is the set of all subsets of X which are not empty.

Laws

$x \notin \emptyset$

$S \subseteq T \Leftrightarrow S \in \mathbb{P}\,T$

$S \subseteq S$ $\neg\,(S \subset S)$

$S \subseteq T \wedge T \subseteq S \Leftrightarrow S = T$ $\neg\,(S \subset T \wedge T \subset S)$

$S \subseteq T \wedge T \subseteq V \Rightarrow S \subseteq V$ $S \subset T \wedge T \subset V \Rightarrow S \subset V$

$\emptyset \subseteq S$ $\emptyset \subset S \Leftrightarrow S \neq \emptyset$

$\mathbb{P}_1 X = \emptyset \Leftrightarrow X = \emptyset$

$X \neq \emptyset \Leftrightarrow X \in \mathbb{P}_1 X$

Name

∪ –   Set union
∩ –   Set intersection
\ –   Set difference

Definition

$$\underline{\quad}[X]\underline{\qquad\qquad\qquad\qquad\qquad\qquad}$$
$$\_\cup\_,\_\cap\_,\_\backslash\_ : \mathbb{P}\,X \times \mathbb{P}\,X \to \mathbb{P}\,X$$

$$\forall S, T : \mathbb{P}\,X \bullet$$
$$S \cup T = \{\, x : X \mid x \in S \lor x \in T \,\} \land$$
$$S \cap T = \{\, x : X \mid x \in S \land x \in T \,\} \land$$
$$S \backslash T = \{\, x : X \mid x \in S \land x \notin T \,\}$$

Description

These are the ordinary operations of set algebra. The members of
the set $S \cup T$ are those objects which are members of S or T or
both. The members of $S \cap T$ are those objects which are members
of both S and T. The members of $S \backslash T$ are those objects which
are members of S but not of T.

Laws

$$S \cup S = S \cup \varnothing = S \cap S = S \backslash \varnothing = S$$
$$S \cap \varnothing = S \backslash S = \varnothing \backslash S = \varnothing$$

$$S \cup T = T \cup S \qquad\qquad S \cap T = T \cap S$$
$$S \cup (T \cup V) = (S \cup T) \cup V \qquad S \cap (T \cap V) = (S \cap T) \cap V$$

$$S \cup (T \cap V) = (S \cup T) \cap (S \cup V)$$
$$S \cap (T \cup V) = (S \cap T) \cup (S \cap V)$$

$$(S \cap T) \cup (S \backslash T) = S$$
$$(S \backslash T) \cap T = \varnothing$$
$$S \backslash (T \backslash V) = (S \backslash T) \cup (S \cap V)$$
$$(S \backslash T) \backslash V = S \backslash (T \cup V)$$

$$S \cup (T \backslash V) = (S \cup T) \backslash (V \backslash S)$$
$$S \cap (T \backslash V) = (S \cap T) \backslash V$$
$$(S \cup T) \backslash V = (S \backslash V) \cup (T \backslash V)$$
$$S \backslash (T \cap V) = (S \backslash T) \cup (S \backslash V)$$

Name

∪ –   Generalized union

∩ –   Generalized intersection

Definition

$$\boxed{\begin{array}{l} =[X]\!\!=\!\!=\!\!=\!\!=\!\!=\!\!=\!\!=\!\!=\!\!=\!\!=\!\!=\!\!=\!\!= \\ \hline \bigcup, \bigcap : \mathbb{P}(\mathbb{P}\,X) \to \mathbb{P}\,X \\ \hline \forall A : \mathbb{P}(\mathbb{P}\,X) \bullet \\ \quad \bigcup A = \{\, x : X \mid (\exists S : A \bullet x \in S) \,\} \wedge \\ \quad \bigcap A = \{\, x : X \mid (\forall S : A \bullet x \in S) \,\} \end{array}}$$

Description

If A is a set of sets, $\bigcup A$ is its *generalized union*: it contains all objects which are members of some member of A. The set $\bigcap A$ is the *generalized intersection* of A: it contains those objects which are members of all members of A.

Laws

$$\bigcup(A \cup B) = (\bigcup A) \cup (\bigcup B)$$
$$\bigcap(A \cup B) = (\bigcap A) \cap (\bigcap B)$$

$$\bigcup[X]\,\varnothing = \varnothing$$
$$\bigcap[X]\,\varnothing = X$$

$$S \cap (\bigcup A) = \bigcup\{\, T : A \bullet S \cap T \,\}$$
$$S \cup (\bigcap A) = \bigcap\{\, T : A \bullet S \cup T \,\}$$
$$(\bigcup A) \setminus S = \bigcup\{\, T : A \bullet T \setminus S \,\}$$
$$S \setminus (\bigcap A) = \bigcup\{\, T : A \bullet S \setminus T \,\}$$
$$A \neq \varnothing \Rightarrow S \setminus (\bigcup A) = \bigcap\{\, T : A \bullet S \setminus T \,\}$$
$$A \neq \varnothing \Rightarrow (\bigcap A) \setminus S = \bigcap\{\, T : A \bullet T \setminus S \,\}$$

$$A \subseteq B \Rightarrow \bigcup A \subseteq \bigcup B$$
$$A \subseteq B \Rightarrow \bigcap B \subseteq \bigcap A$$

Name

first, *second*   –   Projection functions for ordered pairs

Definition

$=[X, Y]$⸺⸺⸺⸺⸺⸺⸺⸺⸺⸺⸺
$first : X \times Y \rightarrow X$
$second : X \times Y \rightarrow Y$
⸺⸺⸺⸺⸺⸺⸺⸺
$\forall x : X; \; y : Y \bullet$
    $first(x, y) = x \; \wedge$
    $second(x, y) = y$

Description

These projection functions split ordered pairs into their first and second co-ordinates.

Laws

$(first \; p, second \; p) = p$

Order properties of set operations

The subset relation $\subseteq$ on sets is a partial order: this is the content of three of the laws shown on its page in the manual. The operations of union and intersection are least upper bound and greatest lower bound operations for this partial order, as is expressed in the laws which follow. If S and T are sets, then $S \cup T$ is the smallest set which contains both S and T as subsets:

$$S \subseteq S \cup T$$
$$T \subseteq S \cup T$$
$$S \subseteq W \land T \subseteq W \Rightarrow S \cup T \subseteq W$$

For a set of sets A, the generalized union $\bigcup A$ is the smallest set which contains each member of A as a subset:

$$\forall S : A \bullet S \subseteq \bigcup A$$
$$(\forall S : A \bullet S \subseteq W) \Rightarrow \bigcup A \subseteq W$$

Similarly, $S \cap T$ is the largest set which is a subset of both S and T:

$$S \cap T \subseteq S$$
$$S \cap T \subseteq T$$
$$W \subseteq S \land W \subseteq T \Rightarrow W \subseteq S \cap T$$

The set $\bigcap A$ is the largest set which is a subset of each member of A:

$$\forall S : A \bullet \bigcap A \subseteq S$$
$$(\forall S : A \bullet W \subseteq S) \Rightarrow W \subseteq \bigcap A$$

Finally, $S \setminus T$ is the largest subset of S which is disjoint from T:

$$S \setminus T \subseteq S$$
$$(S \setminus T) \cap T = \varnothing$$
$$W \subseteq S \land W \cap T = \varnothing \Rightarrow W \subseteq S \setminus T$$

4.2 Relations

Name

↔   –   Binary relations
↦   –   Maplet

Definition

$$X \leftrightarrow Y == \mathbb{P}(X \times Y)$$

┌─[X, Y]─────────────────────────────
│ $\_ \mapsto \_ : X \times Y \to X \times Y$
│ ─────────────────────
│ $\forall x : X;\ y : Y \bullet$
│ $x \mapsto y = (x, y)$
└─────────────────────────────────────

Description

If X and Y are sets, then $X \leftrightarrow Y$ is the set of *binary relations* between X and Y. Each such relation is a subset of $X \times Y$. The 'maplet' notation $x \mapsto y$ is a graphic way of expressing the ordered pair (x, y).

The definition of $X \leftrightarrow Y$ given here repeats the one given on page 88.

Name

dom, ran – Domain and range of a relation

Definition

$$\boxed{\begin{array}{l} =[X, Y] \\ \hline \mathrm{dom} : (X \leftrightarrow Y) \to \mathbb{P}\, X \\ \mathrm{ran} : (X \leftrightarrow Y) \to \mathbb{P}\, Y \\ \hline \forall R : X \leftrightarrow Y \bullet \\ \qquad \mathrm{dom}\, R = \{\, x : X;\ y : Y \mid (x \mapsto y) \in R \bullet x \,\} \wedge \\ \qquad \mathrm{ran}\, R = \{\, x : X;\ y : Y \mid (x \mapsto y) \in R \bullet y \,\} \end{array}}$$

Description

If R is a binary relation between X and Y, then the *domain* of R ($\mathrm{dom}\, R$) is the set of all members of X which are related to at least one member of Y by R. The *range* of R ($\mathrm{ran}\, R$) is the set of all members of Y to which at least one member of X is related by R.

Laws

$$x \in \mathrm{dom}\, R \Leftrightarrow (\exists\, y : Y \bullet (x \mapsto y) \in R)$$
$$y \in \mathrm{ran}\, R \Leftrightarrow (\exists\, x : X \bullet (x \mapsto y) \in R)$$

$$\mathrm{dom}\, \{\, x_1 \mapsto y_1, \ldots, x_n \mapsto y_n \,\} = \{\, x_1, \ldots, x_n \,\}$$
$$\mathrm{ran}\, \{\, x_1 \mapsto y_1, \ldots, x_n \mapsto y_n \,\} = \{\, y_1, \ldots, y_n \,\}$$

$$\mathrm{dom}(S \cup T) = (\mathrm{dom}\, S) \cup (\mathrm{dom}\, T)$$
$$\mathrm{ran}(S \cup T) = (\mathrm{ran}\, S) \cup (\mathrm{ran}\, T)$$
$$\mathrm{dom}(S \cap T) \subseteq (\mathrm{dom}\, S) \cap (\mathrm{dom}\, T)$$
$$\mathrm{ran}(S \cap T) \subseteq (\mathrm{ran}\, S) \cap (\mathrm{ran}\, T)$$

$$\mathrm{dom}\, \varnothing = \varnothing$$
$$\mathrm{ran}\, \varnothing = \varnothing$$

Name

id   –   Identity relation
;   –   Relational composition
o   –   Backward relational composition

Definition

$\mathrm{id}\, X == \{\, x : X \bullet x \mapsto x \,\}$

$$
\begin{array}{l}
=[X, Y, Z]\rule{4cm}{0.4pt} \\
\quad \_\,;\,\_ : (X \leftrightarrow Y) \times (Y \leftrightarrow Z) \rightarrow (X \leftrightarrow Z) \\
\quad \_\,\circ\,\_ : (Y \leftrightarrow Z) \times (X \leftrightarrow Y) \rightarrow (X \leftrightarrow Z) \\
\hline
\quad \forall R : X \leftrightarrow Y;\ S : Y \leftrightarrow Z \bullet \\
\qquad R\,;\,S = S \circ R = \{\, x : X;\ y : Y;\ z : Z \mid \\
\qquad\qquad\qquad (x \mapsto y) \in R \wedge (y \mapsto z) \in S \bullet x \mapsto z \,\}
\end{array}
$$

Description

The *identity relation* $\mathrm{id}\, X$ on a set X relates each member of X to itself. The *composition* $R\,;\,S$ of two relations $R : X \leftrightarrow Y$ and $S : Y \leftrightarrow Z$ relates a member x of X to a member z of Z if and only if there is at least one element y of Y to which x is related by R and which is itself related to z by S. The notation $S \circ R$ is an alternative to $R\,;\,S$.

Laws

$(x \mapsto x') \in \mathrm{id}\, X \Leftrightarrow x = x' \in X$

$(x \mapsto z) \in R\,;\,S \Leftrightarrow (\exists y : Y \bullet (x \mapsto y) \in R \wedge (y \mapsto z) \in S)$

$R\,;\,(S\,;\,T) = (R\,;\,S)\,;\,T$

$\mathrm{id}\, X\,;\,R = R$

$R\,;\,\mathrm{id}\, Y = R$

$\mathrm{id}\, V\,;\,\mathrm{id}\, W = \mathrm{id}(V \cap W)$

$(f \circ g)(x) = f(g(x))$

Name

◁ – Domain restriction
▷ – Range restriction

Definition

$=[X, Y]$

$\_\triangleleft\_ : \mathbb{P}\, X \times (X \leftrightarrow Y) \to (X \leftrightarrow Y)$
$\_\triangleright\_ : (X \leftrightarrow Y) \times \mathbb{P}\, Y \to (X \leftrightarrow Y)$

$\forall S : \mathbb{P}\, X;\ R : X \leftrightarrow Y \bullet$
$\qquad S \triangleleft R = \{\, x : X;\ y : Y \mid x \in S \wedge (x \mapsto y) \in R \bullet x \mapsto y \,\}$
$\forall R : X \leftrightarrow Y;\ T : \mathbb{P}\, Y \bullet$
$\qquad R \triangleright T = \{\, x : X;\ y : Y \mid (x \mapsto y) \in R \wedge y \in T \bullet x \mapsto y \,\}$

Description

The *domain restriction* $S \triangleleft R$ of a relation R to a set S relates x to y if and only if R relates x to y and x is a member of S. The *range restriction* $R \triangleright T$ of R to a set T relates x to y if and only if R relates x to y and y is a member of T.

Laws

$S \triangleleft R = \operatorname{id} S \,\mathring{;}\, R = (S \times Y) \cap R$
$R \triangleright T = R \,\mathring{;}\, \operatorname{id} T = R \cap (X \times T)$

$\operatorname{dom}(S \triangleleft R) = S \cap (\operatorname{dom} R)$
$\operatorname{ran}(R \triangleright T) = (\operatorname{ran} R) \cap T$

$S \triangleleft R \subseteq R$
$R \triangleright T \subseteq R$

$(S \triangleleft R) \triangleright T = S \triangleleft (R \triangleright T)$
$S \triangleleft (V \triangleleft R) = (S \cap V) \triangleleft R$
$(R \triangleright T) \triangleright W = R \triangleright (T \cap W)$

Name

◁ – Domain anti-restriction
▷ – Range anti-restriction

Definition

$$\boxed{\begin{array}{l} \underline{\quad}\,[X,\,Y] \\ \hline \_ \triangleleft \_ : \mathbb{P}\,X \times (X \leftrightarrow Y) \to (X \leftrightarrow Y) \\ \_ \triangleright \_ : (X \leftrightarrow Y) \times \mathbb{P}\,Y \to (X \leftrightarrow Y) \\ \hline \forall S : \mathbb{P}\,X;\ R : X \leftrightarrow Y \bullet \\ \qquad S \triangleleft R = \{\,x : X;\ y : Y \mid x \notin S \wedge (x \mapsto y) \in R \bullet x \mapsto y\,\} \\ \forall R : X \leftrightarrow Y;\ T : \mathbb{P}\,Y \bullet \\ \qquad R \triangleright T = \{\,x : X;\ y : Y \mid (x \mapsto y) \in R \wedge y \notin T \bullet x \mapsto y\,\} \end{array}}$$

Description

These two operations are the complemented counterparts of the
restriction operations $\_ \triangleleft \_$ and $\_ \triangleright \_$. An object x is related to an
object y by the relation $S \triangleleft R$ if and only if x is related to y by R
and x is not a member of S. Similarly, x is related to y by $R \triangleright T$
if and only if x is related to y by R and y is not a member of T.

Laws

$$S \triangleleft R = (X \setminus S) \triangleleft R$$
$$R \triangleright T = R \triangleright (Y \setminus T)$$

$$(S \triangleleft R) \cup (S \triangleleft R) = R$$
$$(R \triangleright T) \cup (R \triangleright T) = R$$

Name

_~_   —   Relational inversion

Definition

$$
\begin{array}{l}
[X, Y] \\
\hline
\_^{\sim} : (X \leftrightarrow Y) \to (Y \leftrightarrow X) \\
\hline
\forall R : X \leftrightarrow Y \bullet \\
\quad R^{\sim} = \{\, x : X;\ y : Y \mid (x \mapsto y) \in R \bullet y \mapsto x \,\}
\end{array}
$$

Notation

The notation R^{-1} is often used for the inverse of R; it is a special case of the notation for iteration (see page 112).

Description

An object y is related to an object x by the *relational inverse* $R^{\sim}$ of R if and only if x is related to y by R.

Laws

$(y \mapsto x) \in R^{\sim} \Leftrightarrow (x \mapsto y) \in R$

$(R^{\sim})^{\sim} = R$

$(R \,\semicolon\, S)^{\sim} = S^{\sim} \,\semicolon\, R^{\sim}$

$(\mathrm{id}\ V)^{\sim} = \mathrm{id}\ V$

$\mathrm{dom}(R^{\sim}) = \mathrm{ran}\ R$

$\mathrm{ran}(R^{\sim}) = \mathrm{dom}\ R$

$\mathrm{id}(\mathrm{dom}\ R) \subseteq R \,\semicolon\, R^{\sim}$

$\mathrm{id}(\mathrm{ran}\ R) \subseteq R^{\sim} \,\semicolon\, R$

Name

$\_(\!|\_|\!)$ – Relational image

Definition

$$
\begin{array}{|l}
\hline
[X, Y] \\
\hline
\_(\!|\_|\!) : (X \leftrightarrow Y) \times \mathbb{P}\,X \rightarrow \mathbb{P}\,Y \\
\hline
\forall R : X \leftrightarrow Y;\ S : \mathbb{P}\,X \bullet \\
\quad R(\!|S|\!) = \{\, x : X;\ y : Y \mid x \in S \land (x \mapsto y) \in R \bullet y \,\} \\
\hline
\end{array}
$$

Description

The *relational image* $R(\!|S|\!)$ of a set S through a relation R is the set of all objects y to which R relates some member x of S.

Laws

$y \in R(\!|S|\!) \Leftrightarrow (\exists x : X \bullet x \in S \land (x \mapsto y) \in R)$

$R(\!|S|\!) = \mathrm{ran}(S \lhd R)$

$\mathrm{dom}(Q \,\fatsemi\, R) = Q^{\sim}(\!|\mathrm{dom}\,R|\!)$

$\mathrm{ran}(Q \,\fatsemi\, R) = R(\!|\mathrm{ran}\,Q|\!)$

$R(\!|S \cup T|\!) = R(\!|S|\!) \cup R(\!|T|\!)$

$R(\!|S \cap T|\!) \subseteq R(\!|S|\!) \cap R(\!|T|\!)$

$R(\!|\mathrm{dom}\,R|\!) = \mathrm{ran}\,R$

$\mathrm{dom}\,R = \mathit{first}(\!|R|\!)$

$\mathrm{ran}\,R = \mathit{second}(\!|R|\!)$

Name

$\_^+$ – Transitive closure
$\_^*$ – Reflexive-transitive closure

Definition

$$
\boxed{\begin{array}{l}
=[X]=\!\!=\!\!=\!\!=\!\!=\!\!=\!\!=\!\!=\!\!=\!\!=\!\!=\!\!=\!\!=\!\!=\!\!=\!\!=\!\!= \\
\_^+, \_^* : (X \leftrightarrow X) \to (X \leftrightarrow X) \\
\hline
\forall R : X \leftrightarrow X \ \bullet \\
\quad R^+ = \bigcap \{\, Q : X \leftrightarrow X \mid R \subseteq Q \wedge Q \,\mathbf{;}\, Q \subseteq Q \,\} \wedge \\
\quad R^* = \bigcap \{\, Q : X \leftrightarrow X \mid \operatorname{id} X \subseteq Q \wedge R \subseteq Q \wedge Q \,\mathbf{;}\, Q \subseteq Q \,\}
\end{array}}
$$

Description

If R is a relation from a set X to itself, R^+ is the strongest or smallest relation containing R which is transitive, and R^* is the strongest relation containing R which is both reflexive and transitive.

For an alternative definition of R^+ and R^* in terms of iteration, see the laws on page 112.

Laws

$R \subseteq R^+$
$R^+ \,\mathbf{;}\, R^+ \subseteq R^+$
$R \subseteq Q \wedge Q \,\mathbf{;}\, Q \subseteq Q \Rightarrow R^+ \subseteq Q$

$\operatorname{id} X \subseteq R^*$
$R \subseteq R^*$
$R^* \,\mathbf{;}\, R^* = R^*$
$\operatorname{id} X \subseteq Q \wedge R \subseteq Q \wedge Q \,\mathbf{;}\, Q \subseteq Q \Rightarrow R^* \subseteq Q$

$R^* = R^+ \cup \operatorname{id} X = (R \cup \operatorname{id} X)^+$
$R^+ = R \,\mathbf{;}\, R^* = R^* \,\mathbf{;}\, R$
$(R^+)^+ = R^+$
$(R^*)^* = R^*$

$S \subseteq R^* (\!| S |\!)$
$R (\!| R^* (\!| S |\!) |\!) \subseteq R^* (\!| S |\!)$
$S \subseteq T \wedge R (\!| T |\!) \subseteq T \Rightarrow R^* (\!| S |\!) \subseteq T$

Monotonic operations

A function $f : \mathbb{P}\, X \to \mathbb{P}\, Y$ is *monotonic* if

$$S \subseteq T \Rightarrow f(S) \subseteq f(T)$$

Many operations on sets and relations are monotonic; for example,

$$Q \subseteq R \Rightarrow Q^+ \subseteq R^+ \wedge Q^* \subseteq R^*$$

The restriction operations are monotonic in each of their arguments:

$$S \subseteq T \wedge Q \subseteq R \Rightarrow S \lhd Q \subseteq T \lhd R$$

A function $f : \mathbb{P}\, X \to \mathbb{P}\, Y$ is monotonic if and only if for all $S,\, T : \mathbb{P}\, X$,

$$f(S \cap T) \subseteq f(S) \cap f(T)$$

Similarly, the function f is monotonic if and only if the following inequality holds for all S and T:

$$f(S) \cup f(T) \subseteq f(S \cup T)$$

If the stronger property

$$f(S \cup T) = f(S) \cup f(T)$$

holds, we say that f is *disjunctive*. Many of the operations on sets and relations are disjunctive:

$$(S \cup T) \cup V = (S \cup V) \cup (T \cup V)$$
$$S \cup (T \cup V) = (S \cup T) \cup (S \cup V)$$
$$(S \cup T) \cap V = (S \cap V) \cup (T \cap V)$$
$$S \cap (T \cup V) = (S \cap T) \cup (S \cap V)$$
$$(S \cup T) \setminus V = (S \setminus V) \cup (T \setminus V)$$
$$\mathrm{dom}(Q \cup R) = (\mathrm{dom}\, Q) \cup (\mathrm{dom}\, R)$$
$$\mathrm{ran}(Q \cup R) = (\mathrm{ran}\, Q) \cup (\mathrm{ran}\, R)$$
$$(P \cup Q)\,\fatsemi\, R = (P\,\fatsemi\, R) \cup (Q\,\fatsemi\, R)$$
$$P\,\fatsemi\,(Q \cup R) = (P\,\fatsemi\, Q) \cup (P\,\fatsemi\, R)$$
$$(S \cup T) \lhd R = (S \lhd R) \cup (T \lhd R)$$
$$S \lhd (Q \cup R) = (S \lhd Q) \cup (S \lhd R)$$
$$R \rhd (S \cup T) = (R \rhd S) \cup (R \rhd T)$$
$$(Q \cup R) \rhd S = (Q \rhd S) \cup (R \rhd S)$$
$$S \ntriangleleft (Q \cup R) = (S \ntriangleleft Q) \cup (S \ntriangleleft R)$$
$$(Q \cup R) \ntriangleright S = (Q \ntriangleright S) \cup (R \ntriangleright S)$$
$$(Q \cup R)^\sim = Q^\sim \cup R^\sim$$
$$(Q \cup R)(\!|S|\!) = Q(\!|S|\!) \cup R(\!|S|\!)$$
$$R(\!|S \cup T|\!) = R(\!|S|\!) \cup R(\!|T|\!)$$

These disjunctive operations are by definition monotonic, so they share all the properties of monotonic functions. Some operations are 'anti-monotonic', in the sense that if $S \subseteq T$ then $f(T) \subseteq f(S)$:

$$S \subseteq T \Rightarrow T \triangleleft R \subseteq S \triangleleft R$$
$$S \subseteq T \Rightarrow R \triangleright T \subseteq R \triangleright S$$
$$T \subseteq V \Rightarrow S \setminus V \subseteq S \setminus T$$

If $f : \mathbb{P} X \to \mathbb{P} X$ monotonic, then Tarski's theorem says that it has a least fixed point S given by

$$S = \bigcap \{ T : \mathbb{P} X \mid f(T) \subseteq T \}$$

This set S has the following two properties:

$$f(S) = S$$
$$\forall T : \mathbb{P} X \mid f(T) \subseteq T \bullet S \subseteq T$$

The first property is that S is a fixed point of f, and the second is that S is included in all 'pre-fixed points' of f: in particular, it is a subset of every other fixed point of f.

4.3 Functions

Name

$\twoheadrightarrow$ – Partial functions
$\rightarrow$ – Total functions

Definition

$X \twoheadrightarrow Y ==$
$\qquad \{ f : X \leftrightarrow Y \mid (\forall x : X; \ y_1, y_2 : Y \bullet$
$\qquad\qquad\qquad (x \mapsto y_1) \in f \wedge (x \mapsto y_2) \in f \Rightarrow y_1 = y_2) \}$
$X \rightarrow Y == \{ f : X \twoheadrightarrow Y \mid \mathrm{dom} f = X \}$

Description

If X and Y are sets, $X \twoheadrightarrow Y$ is the set of *partial functions* from X to Y. These are relations which relate each member x of X to at most one member of Y. This member of Y, if it exists, is written $f x$. $X \rightarrow Y$ is the set of *total functions* from X to Y. These are partial functions with domain X; they relate each member of X to exactly one member of Y.

An alternative definition of $X \rightarrow Y$ was given on page 88. It is equivalent to the one given here.

Laws

$f \in X \twoheadrightarrow Y \Leftrightarrow f \circ f^{\sim} = \mathrm{id}(\mathrm{ran} f)$

Name

$\rightarrowtail\!\!\!\!\rightarrow$ –   Partial injections
$\rightarrowtail$ –   Total injections

Definition

$X \rightarrowtail\!\!\!\!\rightarrow Y ==$
$\qquad \{ f : X \rightarrow\!\!\!\!\rightarrow Y \mid (\forall x_1, x_2 : \mathrm{dom}\, f \bullet f(x_1) = f(x_2) \Rightarrow x_1 = x_2) \}$
$X \rightarrowtail Y == (X \rightarrowtail\!\!\!\!\rightarrow Y) \cap (X \rightarrow Y)$

Description

If X and Y are sets, $X \rightarrowtail\!\!\!\!\rightarrow Y$ is the set of *partial injections* from X to Y. These are partial functions from X to Y which map different elements of the domain to different objects. $X \rightarrowtail Y$ is the set of *total injections* from X to Y, the partial injections which are also total functions.

Laws

$f \in X \rightarrowtail\!\!\!\!\rightarrow Y \Leftrightarrow f \in X \rightarrow\!\!\!\!\rightarrow Y \wedge f^{\sim} \in Y \rightarrow\!\!\!\!\rightarrow X$
$f \in X \rightarrowtail Y \Leftrightarrow f \in X \rightarrow Y \wedge f^{\sim} \in Y \rightarrow\!\!\!\!\rightarrow X$

$f \in X \rightarrowtail\!\!\!\!\rightarrow Y \Rightarrow f(\!|S \cap T|\!) = f(\!|S|\!) \cap f(\!|T|\!)$

Name

↠ – Partial surjections
↠ – Total surjections
⤖ – Bijections

Definition

$$X \twoheadrightarrow Y == \{\, f : X \nrightarrow Y \mid \operatorname{ran} f = Y \,\}$$
$$X \rightarrow Y == (X \twoheadrightarrow Y) \cap (X \to Y)$$
$$X \rightarrowtail Y == (X \to Y) \cap (X \rightarrowtail Y)$$

Description

If X and Y are sets, $X \twoheadrightarrow Y$ is the set of *partial surjections* from X to Y. These are partial functions from X to Y which have the whole of Y as their range. $X \rightarrow Y$ is the set of *total surjections* from X to Y, the functions which have the whole of X as their domain and the whole of Y as their range. $X \rightarrowtail Y$ is the set of *bijections* from X to Y. These map the elements of X onto the elements of Y in a one-to-one correspondence.

Laws

$$f \in X \rightarrowtail Y \Leftrightarrow f \in X \to Y \wedge f^{\sim} \in Y \to X$$
$$f \in X \rightarrowtail Y \Rightarrow f \circ f^{\sim} = \operatorname{id} Y$$

Name

$\oplus$ – Functional overriding

Definition

$\boxed{\begin{array}{l} =[X, Y]\underline{} \\ \hline \_\oplus\_ : (X \nrightarrow Y) \times (X \nrightarrow Y) \to (X \nrightarrow Y) \\ \hline \forall f, g : X \nrightarrow Y \bullet \\ \qquad f \oplus g = ((\mathrm{dom}\, g) \ntriangleleft f) \cup g \end{array}}$

Description

The function $f \oplus g$ is defined on the union of the domains of f and g. On the domain of g it agrees with g, and elsewhere on its domain it agrees with f.

Laws

$f \oplus f = f$

$f \oplus (g \oplus h) = (f \oplus g) \oplus h$

$\varnothing \oplus f = f$

$f \oplus \varnothing = f$

$\mathrm{dom}\, f \cap \mathrm{dom}\, g = \varnothing \Rightarrow f \oplus g = f \cup g$

$x \in (\mathrm{dom}\, f) \setminus (\mathrm{dom}\, g) \Rightarrow (f \oplus g)\, x = f\, x$

$x \in \mathrm{dom}\, g \Rightarrow (f \oplus g)\, x = g\, x$

$\mathrm{dom}(f \oplus g) = (\mathrm{dom}\, f) \cup (\mathrm{dom}\, g)$

$\mathrm{ran}(f \oplus g) = (\mathrm{ran}((\mathrm{dom}\, g) \ntriangleleft f)) \cup (\mathrm{ran}\, g)$

$S \triangleleft (f \oplus g) = (S \triangleleft f) \oplus (S \triangleleft g)$

$(f \oplus g) \triangleright T \subseteq (f \triangleright T) \oplus (g \triangleright T)$

Relational operations on functions

Functions are just a special kind of relation, so the relational operations, such as ∘ and ◁, may be used on functions. Many of these operations yield functions when applied to functions, and some preserve other properties such as injectivity.

The identity relation is a function – in fact, an injection – and composition and restriction map functions to functions:

$$S \subseteq X \Rightarrow \mathrm{id}\, S \in X \rightarrowtail X$$
$$\mathrm{id}\, X \in X \rightarrowtail X$$

$$f \in X \twoheadrightarrow Y \wedge g \in Y \twoheadrightarrow Z \Rightarrow g \circ f \in X \twoheadrightarrow Z$$
$$f \in X \rightarrow Y \wedge g \in Y \twoheadrightarrow Z \wedge \mathrm{ran}\, f \subseteq \mathrm{dom}\, g \Rightarrow g \circ f \in X \rightarrow Z$$

$$f \in X \twoheadrightarrow Y \Rightarrow S \lhd f \in X \twoheadrightarrow Y$$
$$f \in X \twoheadrightarrow Y \Rightarrow f \rhd T \in X \twoheadrightarrow Y$$

The composition of two injections and the restriction of an injection are again injections, and inversion maps injections to injections:

$$f \in X \rightarrowtail Y \wedge g \in Y \rightarrowtail Z \Rightarrow g \circ f \in X \rightarrowtail Z$$
$$f \in X \rightarrowtail Y \Rightarrow S \lhd f \in X \rightarrowtail Y$$
$$f \in X \rightarrowtail Y \Rightarrow f \rhd T \in X \rightarrowtail Y$$
$$f \in X \rightarrowtail Y \Rightarrow f^{\sim} \in Y \rightarrowtail X$$

Finally, set-theoretic operations may be used to combine functions. Note especially that the union of two functions is a function only if they agree on the intersection of their domains:

$$f \in X \twoheadrightarrow Y \wedge g \in X \twoheadrightarrow Y \wedge$$
$$(\mathrm{dom}\, f) \lhd g = (\mathrm{dom}\, g) \lhd f \Rightarrow f \cup g \in X \twoheadrightarrow Y$$

$$f \in X \twoheadrightarrow Y \wedge g \in X \twoheadrightarrow Y \Rightarrow f \cap g \in X \twoheadrightarrow Y$$
$$f \in X \rightarrowtail Y \wedge g \in X \rightarrowtail Y \Rightarrow f \cap g \in X \rightarrowtail Y$$

The last two laws are special cases of the laws that any subset of a function is a function, and any subset of an injection is an injection:

$$f \in X \twoheadrightarrow Y \wedge g \subseteq f \Rightarrow g \in X \twoheadrightarrow Y$$
$$f \in X \rightarrowtail Y \wedge g \subseteq f \Rightarrow g \in X \rightarrowtail Y$$

4.4 Numbers and finiteness

Name

N	–	Natural numbers
Z	–	Integers
$+, -, *, \mathrm{div}, \mathrm{mod}$	–	Arithmetic operations
$<, \leq, \geq, >$	–	Numerical comparison

Definition

[Z]

$$N : \mathbb{P}\, Z$$

$$\_ + \_, \_ - \_, \_ * \_ : Z \times Z \to Z$$
$$\_ \,\mathrm{div}\, \_, \_ \,\mathrm{mod}\, \_ : Z \times (Z \setminus \{0\}) \to Z$$
$$- : Z \to Z$$

$$\_ < \_, \_ \leq \_, \_ \geq \_, \_ > \_ : Z \leftrightarrow Z$$

$$N = \{\, n : Z \mid n \geq 0 \,\}$$
... other definitions omitted ...

Notation

Decimal notation may be used for elements of N. Negative numbers may be written down using the unary minus function $(-)$.

Description

N is the set of *natural numbers* $\{0, 1, 2, \ldots\}$, and Z is the set of integers $\{\ldots, -2, -1, 0, 1, 2, \ldots\}$. The usual *arithmetic operations* of addition, subtraction, multiplication, integer division and modulo are provided. Integer division and the modulo operation use truncation towards minus infinity, so that they together obey the three laws listed below. Numbers may be compared with the usual ordering relations.

Laws

$$b > 0 \Rightarrow 0 \leq a \bmod b < b$$

$$b \neq 0 \Rightarrow a = (a \,\mathrm{div}\, b) * b + a \bmod b$$

$$b \neq 0 \wedge c \neq 0 \Rightarrow (a * c) \,\mathrm{div}\, (b * c) = a \,\mathrm{div}\, b$$

Name

N_1 –   Strictly positive integers
succ   –   Successor function

Definition

$N_1 == N \setminus \{0\}$

$$succ : N \to N$$
$$\forall n : N \bullet succ(n) = n + 1$$

Description

N_1 is the set of *strictly positive integers*; it contains every natural number except 0. If n is a natural number, $succ(n)$ is the next one, namely $n + 1$. If we take *succ* as primitive, it is possible to describe all the operations on numbers in terms of it.

Laws

$succ \in N \rightarrowtail N_1$

Name

R^k –   Iteration

Definition

$$\begin{array}{l}
\underline{[X]}\\
\hline
iter : \mathbb{Z} \to (X \leftrightarrow X) \to (X \leftrightarrow X)\\
\hline
\forall R : X \leftrightarrow X \bullet\\
\quad iter\,0\,R = \operatorname{id} X \;\wedge\\
\quad (\forall k : \mathbb{N} \bullet iter\,(k+1)\,R = R \,\mathbin{\raise.5ex\hbox{$_9^o$}}\, (iter\,k\,R)) \;\wedge\\
\quad (\forall k : \mathbb{N} \bullet iter\,(-k)\,R = iter\,k\,(R^{\sim}))
\end{array}$$

Notation

iter k R is usually written R^k.

Description

Two objects x and y are related by R^k, where $k \geq 0$, if there are $k+1$ objects $x_0, x_1, \ldots, x_k$ with $x = x_0$, $(x_i, x_{i+1}) \in R$ for each i such that $0 \leq i < k$, and $x_k = y$. R^{-k} is defined to be $(R^{\sim})^k$.

Laws

$$R^0 = \operatorname{id} X$$
$$R^1 = R$$
$$R^2 = R \mathbin{\raise.5ex\hbox{$_9^o$}} R$$
$$R^{-1} = R^{\sim}$$
$$k \geq 0 \Rightarrow R^{k+1} = R \mathbin{\raise.5ex\hbox{$_9^o$}} R^k = R^k \mathbin{\raise.5ex\hbox{$_9^o$}} R$$

$$(R^{\sim})^a = (R^a)^{\sim}$$
$$R^{a+b} = R^a \mathbin{\raise.5ex\hbox{$_9^o$}} R^b$$
$$R^{a*b} = (R^a)^b$$

$$R^+ = \bigcup\{\, k : \mathbb{N}_1 \bullet R^k \,\}$$
$$R^* = \bigcup\{\, k : \mathbb{N} \bullet R^k \,\}$$

$$R \mathbin{\raise.5ex\hbox{$_9^o$}} S = S \mathbin{\raise.5ex\hbox{$_9^o$}} R \Rightarrow (R \mathbin{\raise.5ex\hbox{$_9^o$}} S)^a = R^a \mathbin{\raise.5ex\hbox{$_9^o$}} S^a$$

Name

.. – Number range

Definition

$$\_\,..\,\_ : \mathbb{Z} \times \mathbb{Z} \to \mathbb{P}\,\mathbb{Z}$$

$$\forall a, b : \mathbb{Z} \bullet$$
$$a \,..\, b = \{\, k : \mathbb{Z} \mid a \leq k \leq b \,\}$$

Description

If a and b are integers, $a \,..\, b$ is the set of integers between a and b inclusive. If $a > b$ then $a \,..\, b$ is empty.

Laws

$$a > b \Rightarrow a \,..\, b = \varnothing$$
$$a \,..\, a = \{a\}$$
$$a \leq b \wedge c \leq d \Rightarrow b \,..\, c \subseteq a \,..\, d$$

Name

F   –   Finite sets
F_1 –   Non-empty finite sets
–   Number of members of a set

Definition

$F\,X == \{\, S : \mathbb{P}\,X \mid \exists\, n : \mathbb{N} \bullet \exists\, f : 1\mathinner{..}n \to S \bullet \operatorname{ran} f = S \,\}$
$F_1\,X == F\,X \setminus \{\varnothing\}$

$$
\begin{array}{l}
\underline{[X]} \\
\hline
\# : F\,X \to \mathbb{N} \\
\hline
\forall S : F\,X \bullet \\
\qquad \#S = (\mu\, n : \mathbb{N} \mid (\exists\, f : 1\mathinner{..}n \rightarrowtail S \bullet \operatorname{ran} f = S)) \\
\end{array}
$$

Description

A subset S of X is *finite* $(S \in F\,X)$ if and only if the members of S can be counted with some natural number. In this case, there is a unique natural number which counts the members of S without repetition, and this is the *size* $\#S$ of S. The sets in $F_1\,X$ are the non-empty members of $F\,X$: those finite sets S with $\#S > 0$.

Laws

$S \in F\,X \Leftrightarrow (\forall f : S \rightarrowtail S \bullet \operatorname{ran} f = S)$

$\varnothing \in F\,X$

$\forall S : F\,X;\ x : X \bullet S \cup \{x\} \in F\,X$

$\#(S \cup T) = \#S + \#T - \#(S \cap T)$

$F_1\,X = \{\, S : F\,X \mid \#S > 0 \,\}$

Name

↠ – Finite partial functions
⤖ – Finite partial injections

Definition

$$X \nrightarrow Y == \{\, f : X \nrightarrow Y \mid \mathrm{dom}\, f \in \mathbb{F}\, X \,\}$$
$$X \rightarrowtail\!\!\!\!\rightarrow Y == (X \nrightarrow Y) \cap (X \rightarrowtail\!\!\!\!\rightarrow Y)$$

Description

If X and Y are sets, $X \nrightarrow Y$ is the set of *finite partial functions* from X to Y. These are partial functions from X to Y whose domain is a finite subset of X. The set of *finite partial injections* $X \rightarrowtail\!\!\!\!\rightarrow Y$ contains those finite partial functions which are also injections.

Laws

$$X \nrightarrow Y = (X \nrightarrow Y) \cap \mathbb{F}(X \times Y)$$

Name

min, max –   Minimum and maximum of a set of numbers

Definition

$$min : \mathbb{P}_1 \mathbb{Z} \nrightarrow \mathbb{Z}$$
$$max : \mathbb{P}_1 \mathbb{Z} \nrightarrow \mathbb{Z}$$

$$min = \{\, S : \mathbb{P}_1 \mathbb{Z};\; m : \mathbb{Z} \mid$$
$$m \in S \wedge (\forall n : S \bullet m \leq n) \bullet S \mapsto m \,\}$$
$$max = \{\, S : \mathbb{P}_1 \mathbb{Z};\; m : \mathbb{Z} \mid$$
$$m \in S \wedge (\forall n : S \bullet m \geq n) \bullet S \mapsto m \,\}$$

Description

The minimum of a set S of integers is that element of S which is smaller than any other, if any. The maximum of S is that element which is larger than any other, if any.

Laws

$\mathbb{F}_1 \mathbb{Z} \subseteq \text{dom } min$

$\mathbb{F}_1 \mathbb{Z} \subseteq \text{dom } max$

$(\mathbb{P} \, \mathbb{N}) \cap (\text{dom } min) = \mathbb{P}_1 \, \mathbb{N}$

$(\mathbb{P} \, \mathbb{N}) \cap (\text{dom } max) = \mathbb{F}_1 \, \mathbb{N}$

$min(S \cup T) = min\{min \, S, min \, T\}$

$max(S \cup T) = max\{max \, S, max \, T\}$

$min(S \cap T) \geq min \, S$

$max(S \cap T) \leq max \, S$

$a \leq b \Rightarrow min(a \mathinner{..} b) = a \wedge max(a \mathinner{..} b) = b$

$(a \mathinner{..} b) \cap (c \mathinner{..} d) = max\{a, c\} \mathinner{..} min\{b, d\}$

Proof by induction

Mathematical induction provides a method of proving universal properties of natural numbers. To show that a property $P(n)$ holds of all natural numbers n, it is enough to show that

(a1) $P(0)$ holds.

(a2) If $P(n)$ holds for some $n : \mathsf{N}$, so does $P(n+1)$:

$$\forall n : \mathsf{N} \bullet P(n) \Rightarrow P(n+1)$$

A similar proof method may be used to prove that $P(S)$ holds for all finite sets $S : \mathbb{F}\, X$. It is enough to show that

(b1) $P(\varnothing)$ holds.

(b2) If $P(S)$ holds then $P(S \cup \{x\})$ holds also:

$$\forall S : \mathbb{F}\, X;\ x : X \bullet P(S) \Rightarrow P(S \cup \{x\})$$

A more powerful proof method for the natural numbers is to assume as hypothesis not just that the immediately preceding number has the property P, but that all smaller numbers do. To establish the theorem $\forall n : \mathsf{N} \bullet P(n)$ by this method, it is enough to show the single fact

(c1) If for all $k < n, P(k)$ holds, so does $P(n)$:

$$\forall n : \mathsf{N} \bullet (\forall k : \mathsf{N} \mid k < n \bullet P(k)) \Rightarrow P(n)$$

There is no need for a separate case for $n = 0$, because proving (c1) entails proving $P(0)$ under no assumptions, for there is no natural number k satisfying $k < 0$.

Analogously, a more powerful proof method for sets requires that a property P be proved to hold of a finite set under the hypothesis that it holds of all *proper* subsets. To establish $\forall S : \mathbb{F}\, X \bullet P(S)$, it is enough to show:

(d1) $\forall S : \mathbb{F}\, X \bullet (\forall T : \mathbb{F}\, X \mid T \subset S \bullet P(T)) \Rightarrow P(S)$

Again, since the empty set has no proper subsets, there is no need for a separate case for $S = \varnothing$.

4.5 Sequences

Name

seq	–	Finite sequences
seq_1	–	Non-empty finite sequences
iseq	–	Injective sequences

Definition

$$seq\,X == \{\, f : \mathsf{N} \nrightarrow X \mid \mathrm{dom}\,f = 1 \mathinner{..} \#f \,\}$$
$$seq_1\,X == \{\, f : seq\,X \mid \#f > 0 \,\}$$
$$iseq\,X == seq\,X \cap (\mathsf{N} \rightarrowtail X)$$

Notation

We write $\langle a_1, \ldots, a_n \rangle$ as a shorthand for the set

$$\{1 \mapsto a_1, \ldots, n \mapsto a_n\}$$

The empty sequence $\langle\rangle$ is an alternative notation for the empty function $\varnothing$ from N to X.

Description

$seq\,X$ is the set of finite sequences over X. These are finite functions from N to X whose domain is a segment $1 \mathinner{..} n$ for some natural number n. $seq_1\,X$ is the set of all finite sequences over X except the empty sequence $\langle\rangle$.

$iseq\,X$ is the set of injective finite sequences over X: these are precisely the finite sequences over X which contain no repetitions.

Laws

$$seq_1\,X = seq\,X \setminus \{\langle\rangle\}$$

Name

$\frown$ – Concatenation

Definition

$$[X]$$

$\_ \frown \_ : \operatorname{seq} X \times \operatorname{seq} X \to \operatorname{seq} X$

$\forall s, t : \operatorname{seq} X \bullet$
$\quad s \frown t = s \cup \{\, n : \operatorname{dom} t \bullet n + \#s \mapsto t(n) \,\}$

Description

For sequences s and t, $s \frown t$ is the *concatenation* of s and t. It contains the elements of s followed by the elements of t.

Laws

$(s \frown t) \frown u = s \frown (t \frown u)$

$\langle\rangle \frown s = s$

$s \frown \langle\rangle = s$

$\#(s \frown t) = \#s + \#t$

Name

$head, last, tail, front$ – Sequence decomposition

Definition

$$
\begin{array}{l}
\rule{6cm}{0.4pt}\,[X]\rule{6cm}{0.4pt} \\
head, last : \mathrm{seq}_1 X \rightarrow X \\
tail, front : \mathrm{seq}_1 X \rightarrow \mathrm{seq}\, X \\
\hline
\forall s : \mathrm{seq}_1 X \bullet \\
\quad head\, s = s(1) \wedge \\
\quad last\, s = s(\#s) \wedge \\
\quad tail\, s = (\lambda\, n : 1 \mathinner{\ldotp\ldotp} \#s - 1 \bullet s(n+1)) \wedge \\
\quad front\, s = (1 \mathinner{\ldotp\ldotp} \#s - 1) \lhd s
\end{array}
$$

Description

For a non-empty sequence s, *head s* and *last s* are the first and last elements of s respectively. The sequences *tail s* and *front s* contain all the elements of s except for the first and except for the last respectively.

Laws

$head(\langle x \rangle \frown s) = x$

$tail(\langle x \rangle \frown s) = s$

$last(s \frown \langle x \rangle) = x$

$front(s \frown \langle x \rangle) = s$

$s \neq \langle\rangle \Rightarrow \langle head\, s \rangle \frown (tail\, s) = s$

$s \neq \langle\rangle \Rightarrow (front\, s) \frown \langle last\, s \rangle = s$

Name

rev – Reverse

Definition

$$\begin{array}{l} =\!\![X]\!\!=\!\!=\!\!=\!\!=\!\!=\!\!=\!\!=\!\!=\!\!=\!\!= \\ rev : \operatorname{seq} X \to \operatorname{seq} X \\ \hline \forall s : \operatorname{seq} X \bullet \\ \quad rev\, s = (\lambda\, n : \operatorname{dom} s \bullet s(\#s - n + 1)) \end{array}$$

Description

If s is a sequence, *rev* s is the sequence containing the same elements as s, but in reverse order.

Laws

$rev\, \langle\rangle = \langle\rangle$

$rev\, \langle x\rangle = \langle x\rangle$

$rev(s \frown t) = (rev\, t) \frown (rev\, s)$

$s \neq \langle\rangle \Rightarrow head(rev\, s) = last\, s \wedge tail(rev\, s) = front\, s$

$s \neq \langle\rangle \Rightarrow last(rev\, s) = head\, s \wedge front(rev\, s) = tail\, s$

$rev(rev\, s) = s$

Name

$\upharpoonright$ – Filtering

Definition

$$\boxed{\begin{array}{l} [X] \\ \hline \_ \upharpoonright \_ : \operatorname{seq} X \times \mathbb{P}\, X \to \operatorname{seq} X \\ \hline \forall V : \mathbb{P}\, X \bullet \\ \quad \langle \rangle \upharpoonright V = \langle \rangle \;\wedge \\ \quad (\forall x : X \bullet \\ \qquad (x \in V \Rightarrow \langle x \rangle \upharpoonright V = \langle x \rangle) \;\wedge \\ \qquad (x \notin V \Rightarrow \langle x \rangle \upharpoonright V = \langle \rangle)) \;\wedge \\ \quad (\forall s, t : \operatorname{seq} X \bullet \\ \qquad (s \frown t) \upharpoonright V = (s \upharpoonright V) \frown (t \upharpoonright V)) \end{array}}$$

Description

If s is a sequence and V is a set, $s \upharpoonright V$ is a sequence which contains just those elements of s which are members of V, in the same order as in s.

Laws

$\operatorname{ran} s \subseteq V \Leftrightarrow s \upharpoonright V = s$

$s \upharpoonright \varnothing = \langle \rangle$

$\#(s \upharpoonright V) \leq \#s$

$(rev\; s) \upharpoonright V = rev(s \upharpoonright V)$

$(s \upharpoonright V) \upharpoonright W = s \upharpoonright (V \cap W)$

Relational operations on sequences

Sequences are a special kind of function – the ones with domain $1 \mathinner{.\,.} k$ for some k – and functions are a special kind of relation, so operations defined on relations may be used on sequences.

If $s : \operatorname{seq} X$ and $f : X \to Y$, then $f \circ s \in \operatorname{seq} Y$ – it is the sequence with the same length as s whose elements are the images of corresponding elements of s under f:

$$\#(f \circ s) = \#s$$
$$\forall i : 1 \mathinner{.\,.} \#s \bullet (f \circ s)(i) = f(s(i))$$

$$f \circ \langle \rangle = \langle \rangle$$
$$f \circ \langle x \rangle = \langle f(x) \rangle$$
$$f \circ (s \mathbin{^\frown} t) = (f \circ s) \mathbin{^\frown} (f \circ t)$$

Another useful relational operation for sequences is 'ran'. The range ran s of a sequence s is just the set of objects which are elements of the sequence:

$$\operatorname{ran} s = \{\, i : 1 \mathinner{.\,.} \#s \bullet s(i) \,\}$$

$$\operatorname{ran} \langle \rangle = \varnothing$$
$$\operatorname{ran} \langle x \rangle = \{ x \}$$
$$\operatorname{ran}(s \mathbin{^\frown} t) = (\operatorname{ran} s) \cup (\operatorname{ran} t)$$

These operations interact with sequence operations such as rev and $\upharpoonright$ in the expected way:

$$rev(f \circ s) = f \circ (rev\, s)$$
$$\operatorname{ran}(rev\, s) = \operatorname{ran} s$$

$$(f \circ s) \upharpoonright V = f \circ (s \upharpoonright f^{\sim}\!(\!|V|\!))$$
$$\operatorname{ran}(s \upharpoonright V) = (\operatorname{ran} s) \cap V$$

Name

$^\frown\!/$ – Distributed concatenation

Definition

$$\begin{array}{|l|}\hline [X] \\ \hline \;\; ^\frown\!/ : \mathrm{seq(seq}\,X\,) \to \mathrm{seq}\,X \\ \hline \;\; ^\frown\!/\langle\rangle = \langle\rangle \\ \;\; \forall s : \mathrm{seq}\,X \bullet \; ^\frown\!/\langle s\rangle = s \\ \;\; \forall q, r : \mathrm{seq(seq}\,X\,) \bullet \\ \qquad ^\frown\!/(q \mathbin{^\frown} r) = (^\frown\!/\,q) \mathbin{^\frown} (^\frown\!/\,r) \\ \hline \end{array}$$

Description

If q is a sequence of sequences, $^\frown\!/\,q$ is the result of concatenating all the elements of q, one after another.

Laws

$$^\frown\!/\langle s, t\rangle = s \mathbin{^\frown} t$$

The following four laws show the interaction of $^\frown\!/$ with rev, $\restriction$, $\circ$ and 'ran':

$$rev(^\frown\!/\,q) = \;^\frown\!/(rev(rev \circ q))$$

The expression on the right of this law can be evaluated by reversing each sequence in q, reversing the resulting sequence of sequences, then concatenating the result with $^\frown\!/$.

$$(^\frown\!/\,q) \restriction V = \;^\frown\!/((\lambda s : \mathrm{seq}\,X \bullet s \restriction V) \circ q)$$

On the right-hand side, each sequence in q is filtered by V, and the results are concatenated.

$$f \circ (^\frown\!/\,q) = \;^\frown\!/((\lambda s : \mathrm{seq}\,X \bullet f \circ s) \circ q)$$

On the right-hand side of this law, f is composed with each sequence in q, and the results are concatenated.

$$\begin{aligned} \mathrm{ran}(^\frown\!/\,q) &= \bigcup\{\, i : 1 \mathinner{\ldotp\ldotp} \#q \bullet \mathrm{ran}(q(i))\,\} \\ &= \bigcup(\mathrm{ran}(\mathrm{ran} \circ q)) \end{aligned}$$

The first expression on the right is the union of the ranges of the individual elements of q. The second expression is a shorter way of saying the same thing.

Name

disjoint   –   Disjointness
partition   –   Partitions

Definition

$$\boxed{\begin{array}{l} =[I, X] \rule{4cm}{0pt} \\[4pt] \mathrm{disjoint}\ \_ : \mathbb{P}\,(I \twoheadrightarrow \mathbb{P}\,X) \\ \_\ \mathrm{partition}\ \_ : (I \twoheadrightarrow \mathbb{P}\,X) \leftrightarrow \mathbb{P}\,X \\[6pt] \hline \\[-6pt] \forall S : I \twoheadrightarrow \mathbb{P}\,X;\ T : \mathbb{P}\,X \bullet \\ \quad (\mathrm{disjoint}\ S \Leftrightarrow \\ \qquad (\forall\, i, j : \mathrm{dom}\,S \mid i \neq j \bullet S(i) \cap S(j) = \varnothing)) \wedge \\ \quad (S\ \mathrm{partition}\ T \Leftrightarrow \\ \qquad \mathrm{disjoint}\ S \wedge \bigcup\{\, i : \mathrm{dom}\,S \bullet S(i)\,\} = T) \end{array}}$$

Description

An indexed family of sets S is *disjoint* if and only if each pair of sets $S(i)$ and $S(j)$ for $i \neq j$ have empty intersection. The family S *partitions* a set T if, in addition, the union of all the sets $S(i)$ is T. A particularly common example of an indexed family of sets is a sequence of sets, which is at base only a function defined on a subset of $\mathbb{N}$.

Laws

disjoint $\varnothing$

disjoint $\langle A \rangle$

disjoint $\langle A, B \rangle \Leftrightarrow A \cap B = \varnothing$

$\langle A, B \rangle$ partition $C \Leftrightarrow A \cap B = \varnothing \wedge A \cup B = C$

Induction for sequences

Proof by induction is valid for natural numbers and for finite sets because every natural number can be reached from zero by repeatedly adding one, and every finite set can be reached from the empty set by repeatedly inserting new members. There are two 'generation principles' like this for sequences, and they correspond to two slightly different styles of proof by induction. First, any sequence can be reached from the empty sequence by repeatedly extending it with new elements. So to prove that a property $P(s)$ holds of all finite sequences $s : \operatorname{seq} X$, it is enough to show that

(a1) $P(\langle\rangle)$ holds.

(a2) If $P(s)$ holds for some sequence s, then $P(s \cap \langle x \rangle)$ holds also:

$$\forall s : \operatorname{seq} X;\ x : X \bullet P(s) \Rightarrow P(s \cap \langle x \rangle)$$

A variant of this style of induction builds up sequences from the back instead of from the front: (a2) may be replaced by

(a2′) If $P(s)$ holds for some sequence s, then $P(\langle x \rangle \cap s)$ holds also:

$$\forall x : X;\ s : \operatorname{seq} X \bullet P(s) \Rightarrow P(\langle x \rangle \cap s)$$

A second way of building up sequences is to start with the empty sequence $\langle\rangle$ and singleton sequences $\langle x \rangle$, and to obtain longer sequences by concatenating shorter ones. So to prove $\forall s : \operatorname{seq} X \bullet P(s)$, it is enough to prove that

(b1) $P(\langle\rangle)$ holds.

(b2) $P(\langle x \rangle)$ holds for all $x : X$.

(b3) If $P(s)$ and $P(t)$ hold, so does $P(s \cap t)$:

$$\forall s, t : \operatorname{seq} X \bullet P(s) \wedge P(t) \Rightarrow P(s \cap t)$$

Although, on the face of it, proofs in this style are more long-winded because there are three cases instead of two, in practice it often leads to more elegant proofs than the first one. For example, the sequence operations *rev*, ⌈, and ⌢/ obey three laws of this form, as do the actions of ran and ∘ on sequences, so proofs about them fit naturally into this style, and there is no need to break the symmetry in favour of the first element or the last, as the other style would require.

4.6 Bags

Name

bag	–	Bags
count	–	Multiplicity
in	–	Bag membership

Definition

$\text{bag}\,X == X \nrightarrow \mathsf{N}_1$

$$
\begin{array}{|l}
\hline
[X] \\\hline
count : \text{bag}\,X \nrightarrow (X \to \mathsf{N}) \\
\_\,\text{in}\,\_ : X \leftrightarrow \text{bag}\,X \\\hline
\forall x : X;\ B : \text{bag}\,X \bullet \\
\qquad count\,B = (\lambda x : X \bullet 0) \oplus B \wedge \\
\qquad x \text{ in } B \Leftrightarrow x \in \text{dom}\,B \\\hline
\end{array}
$$

Notation

We write $[\![a_1, \ldots, a_n]\!]$ for the bag

$$\{a_1 \mapsto k_1, \ldots, a_n \mapsto k_n\}$$

where for each i, the element a_i appears k_i times in the list a_1, ..., a_n. The empty bag $[\![\,]\!]$ is a notation for the empty function $\varnothing$ from X to N.

Description

$\text{bag}\,X$ is the set of *bags* of elements of X. These are collections of elements of X in which the number of times an element occurs is significant. The number of times x appears in the bag B is *count B x*, and the relationship x in B holds exactly if this number is greater than zero.

Laws

$x \text{ in } B \Leftrightarrow count\,B\,x > 0$

$\text{dom}\,[\![a_1, \ldots, a_n]\!] = \{a_1, \ldots, a_n\}$

Name

⊎ –   Bag union

Definition

$$
\begin{array}{|l}
\hline
[X] \\
\hline
\_ \uplus \_ : \operatorname{bag} X \times \operatorname{bag} X \to \operatorname{bag} X \\
\hline
\forall B, C : \operatorname{bag} X; \ x : X \bullet \\
\quad count\,(B \uplus C)\,x = count\,B\,x + count\,C\,x \\
\hline
\end{array}
$$

Description

$B \uplus C$ is the *bag union* of B and C. The number of times any object appears in $B \uplus C$ is the sum of the number of times it appears in B and in C.

Laws

$\operatorname{dom}(B \uplus C) = \operatorname{dom} B \cup \operatorname{dom} C$

$[\![\,]\!] \uplus B = B \uplus [\![\,]\!] = B$

$B \uplus C = C \uplus B$

$(B \uplus C) \uplus D = B \uplus (C \uplus D)$

Name

items – Bag of elements of a sequence

Definition

$$=[X]=$$
$$items : \operatorname{seq} X \to \operatorname{bag} X$$

$$\forall s : \operatorname{seq} X; \ x : X \bullet$$
$$count\,(items\,s)\,x = \#\{\,i : \operatorname{dom} s \mid s(i) = x\,\}$$

Description

If s is a sequence, *items s* is the bag in which each element x appears exactly as often as x appears in s.

Laws

$$\operatorname{dom}(items\,s) = \operatorname{ran} s$$

$$items\,\langle a_1, \ldots, a_n \rangle = [\![a_1, \ldots, a_n]\!]$$

$$items(s \frown t) = items\,s \uplus items\,t$$

$$items\,s = items\,t \Leftrightarrow$$
$$(\exists f : \operatorname{dom} s \rightarrowtail \operatorname{dom} t \bullet s = t \circ f)$$

CHAPTER FIVE

Sequential Systems

The Z language described in Chapter 3 is a system of notation for building structured mathematical theories, and the library of definitions in Chapter 4 provides a vocabulary for that language; but neither has any necessary connection with computer programming. Even the most complex Z specification is, from one point of view, nothing more than a mathematical theory with a certain structure. This chapter explains the conventions which allow us to use these structured mathematical theories to describe computer programs. It concentrates on sequential, imperative programming, explaining how schemas describe the state space and operations of abstract data types. It also explains rules for proving that one abstract data type is implemented by another.

5.1 States and operations

An abstract data type consists of a set of *states*, called the *state space*, a non-empty set of *initial states*, and a number of *operations*. Each operation has certain input and output variables, and is specified by a relationship between the input and output variables and a pair of states, one representing the state before the execution of the operation, and the other representing the state after execution.

In Z, the set of states of an abstract data type is specified by a schema, which is conventionally given the same name as the data type itself: for example, the specification of a birthday book in Chapter 1 has a schema *BirthdayBook* describing its state space. By convention, none of the components of the state space schema has any decoration. As another example, the following schema defines the state space of a simple counter with a current value and a limit:

```
┌─ Counter ──────────────────────────────────────────
│ value, limit : N
├────────────────────────────────────────────────────
│ value ≤ limit
└────────────────────────────────────────────────────
```

Here the state space is the set { *Counter* • *θCounter* } of bindings having two components *value* and *limit* with $0 \leq value \leq limit$. All states of the system obey this invariant relationship documented by the declaration of *value* and *limit* and by the predicate part of the schema.

The set of initial states of an abstract data type is specified by another schema with the same signature as the state space schema. The abstract data type may start in any one of the initial states; often there is only one of them. Here is a schema describing an initial state for the counter:

```
┌─ InitCounter ──────────────────────────────────────
│ Counter
├────────────────────────────────────────────────────
│ value = 0
│ limit = 100
└────────────────────────────────────────────────────
```

For a specification to describe a genuine abstract data type, there must be at least one possible initial state. In the example, this is expressed by the theorem

$\exists$ *Counter* • *InitCounter*

The operations of an abstract data type are specified by schemas which have all the components of both *State* and *State'*, where *State* is the schema describing the state space. The state of the abstract data type before the operation is modelled by the undashed components of its schema, and the state afterwards is modelled by the components decorated with a dash. As an example, here is an operation which increments the value of the counter by one:

```
┌─ Inc ──────────────────────────────────────────────
│ Counter
│ Counter'
├────────────────────────────────────────────────────
│ value' = value + 1
│ limit' = limit
└────────────────────────────────────────────────────
```

Because of the meaning of schema inclusion (see Section 3.4), the properties of *Counter* and *Counter'* are implicitly part of the property of this schema: it is implicitly part of the specification of the operation that the invariant relationship holds before and after it.

The property of this schema is a relationship between the state before the operation and the state after it: this relationship holds when the invariant is satisfied by both these states, and they are related by the two predicates in the body of *Inc*. Here is how this relationship can be understood as specifying a program. Think of a state before the operation is executed; if the state is related to at least one possible state after the operation, then the operation must terminate successfully, and the state after the operation must be one of those related to the state before it. If the predicate relates the state before the operation to no state afterwards, then nothing is guaranteed: the operation may fail to terminate, may terminate abnormally, or may terminate successfully in any state at all.

The condition that there should exist a possible state after the operation related to the state before it is called the *pre-condition* of the operation. If *Op* is a schema describing an operation on a state space *State*, then pre *Op* is a schema describing its pre-condition: if *Op* has no inputs or outputs, pre *Op* is equivalent to the schema

$$\exists\, State' \bullet Op$$

This has the same signature as *State*, but its property is the pre-condition of the operation *Op*. The pre-condition schema pre *Inc* of the operation *Inc* is

---
Counter

$\exists\, Counter' \bullet$
  $value' = value + 1 \;\wedge$
  $limit' = limit$

The state after the operation is implicitly required to satisfy the invariant, and the predicate in this schema is logically equivalent to

$$\exists\, value', limit' : \mathbb{N} \mid value' \leq limit' \bullet$$
$$value' = value + 1 \wedge limit' = limit$$

or to $value + 1 \leq limit$. This means that *value* must be strictly less than *limit* for the success of *Inc* to be guaranteed. It is a useful check on the accuracy of a specification to make such *implicit pre-conditions* explicit and check them against the expected pre-condition. Also, the state before the operation is required to satisfy the invariant: the specification of *Inc* implicitly includes the fact that *Inc* need not behave properly if started in an invalid state.

As well as states before and after execution, operations can have inputs and outputs. The inputs are modelled by components of the schema decorated with ?, and the outputs by components decorated with !. Here is an operation which adds its input to the value of the counter, and outputs the new value:

```
__Add_____
  Counter
  Counter'
  jump? : N
  new_value! : N
_____
  value' = value + jump?
  limit' = limit
  new_value! = value'
```

This operation is guaranteed to terminate successfully, provided the state before execution and the input satisfy the implicit pre-condition that $value + jump? \leq limit$. If this pre-condition is satisfied, then the state after execution and the output will satisfy the relationship specified in the body of the schema. The schema operator 'pre' is also defined for operations with inputs and outputs. If Op has the input $x? : X$ and the output $y! : Y$, then pre Op is the schema

$$\exists State'; \; y! : Y \bullet Op$$

whose components are the state variables from *State*, together with the input $x?$. The pre-condition pre *Add* schema for *Add* is the schema

```
_____
  Counter
  jump? : N
_____
  ∃ Counter'; new_value! : N •
      value' = value + jump?
      limit' = limit
      new_value! = value'
```

The predicate part of this schema is logically equivalent to the implicit pre-condition $value + jump? \leq limit$.

Both the operations *Inc* and *Add* have the property that the state after the operation and the output are completely determined by the state before the operation and the input, but this need not be the case. It is possible to specify *non-deterministic* operations, in which the state before the operation and the input determine a range of possible outputs and states after the operation. Non-deterministic operations are important because they sometimes allow specifications to be made simpler and more abstract.

5.2 The Δ and Ξ conventions

Operations on data types are specified by schemas which have two copies of the state variables among their components: an undecorated set corresponding to the state of the data type before the operation, and a dashed set corresponding to the state after the operation. To make it more convenient to declare these variables, there is a convention that whenever a schema *State* is introduced as the state space of an abstract data type, the schema $\Delta State$ is implicitly defined as the combination of *State* and *State'*, unless a different definition is made explicitly:

$$
\begin{array}{|l}
\hline
\_\Delta State \underline{\hspace{4cm}} \\
\quad State \\
\quad State' \\
\hline
\end{array}
$$

With this definition, each operation on the data type can be specified by extending $\Delta State$ with declarations of the inputs and outputs of the operation and predicates giving the pre-condition and post-condition.

The character Δ is just a letter in the name of this schema, and the implicit definition of $\Delta State$ is no more than a convention. In many specifications, a different definition is given to $\Delta State$: for example, the state of the data type may contain a count of the number of operations performed so far, and the fact that it is incremented at each operation could be made part of $\Delta State$, rather than repeating it for each operation specified.

Many data types have operations which access information in the state without changing the state at all. This fact can be recorded by including the equation $\theta State = \theta State'$ in the post-condition of the operation, but it is convenient to have a special schema $\Xi State$ on which these access operations can be built. Like $\Delta State$, the schema $\Xi State$ is implicitly defined whenever a schema *State* is introduced as the state space of a data type:

$$
\begin{array}{|l}
\hline
\_\Xi State \underline{\hspace{4cm}} \\
\quad \Delta State \\
\hline
\quad \theta State = \theta State' \\
\hline
\end{array}
$$

Again, this definition may be overridden by an explicit definition of

$\Xi State$: if, for example, a record were being kept of the number of operations performed on the system, $\Xi State$ might say that no part of the state changed except the count.

5.3 Loose specifications

The schemas which define the state space and operations of an abstract data type may refer to global variables of the specification, and (as discussed in Section 2.3.2) there may be more than one situation which satisfies the global property of the specification. In other words, the predicates which constrain the global variables may not completely fix their values. We call specifications in which this happens *loose* specifications. The same kind of thing occurs with specifications which introduce new basic types by the mechanism described in Section 3.2.1, because the specification does not fix what objects are members of the basic types.

There are several circumstances where loose specifications and new basic types are useful:

- The specification may describe in detail only some aspects of a system, but need to mention other things not specified in detail. For example, a text editor needs to deal with characters, and it might treat blanks specially; but the specification need not say precisely what characters there are, except that one of them is the blank character.

- There may be constants of a system which must be chosen by the implementor. For example, a filing system may encode its directory information in data blocks, and this encoding must be constant, but it can be chosen by the implementor of the filing system.

- There may be parameters of a system chosen when the system is configured. For example, an operating system may run on machine configurations with any number of disk drives, and the implementor must allow the number to be chosen when the operating system is configured.

Whatever use is made of loose specifications, they provide a way to describe a *family* of abstract data types. Each situation which satisfies the global property of the specification identifies one member of the family. In some cases it is up to the implementor to choose one member of the family and implement it; in other cases, the choice is forced by information outside the formal specification; and sometimes all the members of the family must be implemented, so that one of them can be chosen later. In all these cases, the formal specification describes the range of members in the family, but the way the choice is made is outside its scope.

5.4 Sequential composition

If $Op1$ and $Op2$ are schemas describing two operations, then $Op1 \,\semi\, Op2$ is a schema which describes their *sequential composition*. For it to be defined, the primed components of $Op1$ representing the state after it must correspond exactly with the undecorated components of $Op2$ representing the state before it, and any inputs or outputs shared by $Op1$ and $Op2$ must have the same types in both of them. The components of $Op1 \,\semi\, Op2$ are the undecorated components of $Op1$ and the primed components of $Op2$, together with their merged inputs and outputs. The formal definition of $Op1 \,\semi\, Op2$ is given on page 77.

Some care is needed in the case of non-deterministic operations, for the meaning of $Op1 \,\semi\, Op2$ then differs from the meaning that would be natural in a programming language, in that its pre-condition is more liberal. In $Op1 \,\semi\, Op2$, the state in which $Op1$ finishes is chosen, if possible, to satisfy the pre-condition of $Op2$, so the pre-condition of $Op1 \,\semi\, Op2$ requires only the existence of a possible intermediate state. In programming, the pre-condition would require that *every* possible state after $Op1$ should satisfy the pre-condition of $Op2$. For $Op1 \,\semi\, Op2$ to be correctly implemented by the program '$Op1; \; Op2$', the following condition must hold:

$$\forall STATE'' \bullet$$
$$(\exists Op1 \bullet \theta STATE' = \theta STATE'')$$
$$\Rightarrow (\exists Op2 \bullet \theta STATE = \theta STATE'')$$

If $Op1$ and $Op2$ share any outputs, $Op1 \,\semi\, Op2$ specifies that the same values should be produced as output by both operations; there is no direct way of achieving this in a program.

Returning to the counter example, $Inc \,\semi\, Inc$ describes an operation which adds 2 to the value of the counter. The operation $Inc \,\semi\, Add$ adds one more than its input, producing the new value as output. It is the schema

$$
\begin{array}{|l}
\hline
\Delta\,Counter \\
jump? : \mathsf{N} \\
new\_value! : \mathsf{N} \\
\hline
value' = value + jump? + 1 \\
limit' = limit \\
new\_value! = value' \\
\hline
\end{array}
$$

In contrast, *Add* $\,\S\,$ *Inc* has the same effect, but its output is one less than the final value of the counter:

$$
\begin{array}{|l}
\hline
\Delta\,Counter \\
jump? : \mathsf{N} \\
new\_value! : \mathsf{N} \\
\hline
value' = value + jump? + 1 \\
limit' = limit \\
new\_value! = value + jump? \\
\hline
\end{array}
$$

This is because the output now comes from the first of the two operations, and is produced before the final increment.

5.5 Operation refinement

When a program is developed from a specification, two sorts of design decision usually need to be taken: the operations described by predicates in the specification must be implemented by algorithms expressed in a programming language, and the data described by mathematical data types in the specification must be implemented by data structures of the programming language.

This section contains the rules for simple *operation refinement*. This allows us to show that one operation is a correct implementation of another operation with the same state space, when both operations are specified by schemas. This is the simplest kind of refinement of one operation by another, and it needs to be extended in two directions to make it generally useful in program development. One of these directions, the introduction of programming language constructs, is outside the scope of this book. The other direction, *data refinement*, by which computer-oriented data structures can be introduced, is the subject of Section 5.6.

If a concrete operation *Cop* is an operation refinement of an abstract operation *Aop*, there are two ways they can differ. The pre-condition of *Cop* may be more liberal than the pre-condition of *Aop*, so that *Cop* is guaranteed to terminate for more states than is *Aop*. Also, *Cop* may be more deterministic than *Aop*, in that for some states before the operation, the range of possible states afterwards may be smaller. But *Cop* must be guaranteed to terminate whenever *Aop* is, and if *Aop* is guaranteed to terminate, then every state which *Cop* might produce must be one of those which *Aop* might produce.

Here is the first of these conditions expressed as a predicate. The schema *State* is the state space of the abstract data type, and *Aop* and *Cop* are operations with an input $x? : X$ and an output $y! : Y$.

$$\forall State;\ x? : X \bullet \text{pre}\ Aop \Rightarrow \text{pre}\ Cop$$

This predicate uses the pre-condition operator 'pre', but it can also be expressed directly in terms of the existential quantifier $\exists$:

$$\forall State;\ x? : X \bullet$$
$$(\exists State';\ y! : Y \bullet Aop) \Rightarrow (\exists State';\ y! : Y \bullet Cop)$$

If the pre-condition of *Aop* is satisfied, then every result which *Cop* might produce must be a possible result of *Aop*. This is expressed by the following predicate:

$$\forall State;\ State';\ x? : X;\ y! : Y \bullet$$
$$\text{pre}\ Aop \wedge Cop \Rightarrow Aop$$

Again this can be expressed without using 'pre':

$$\forall State;\ x? : X \bullet$$
$$(\exists State';\ y! : Y \bullet Aop) \Rightarrow$$
$$(\forall State';\ y! : Y \bullet Cop \Rightarrow Aop)$$

If these two conditions are satisfied, then the concrete operation is suitable for all purposes for which the abstract operation was suitable. If the abstract operation could be relied upon to terminate, then so can the concrete operation. This is the content of the first condition. Also, if the abstract operation could be relied on to produce a state after execution which had a certain property, then so can the concrete operation, because the second condition guarantees that all the states which might be reached by the concrete operation can also be reached by the abstract operation.

5.6 Data refinement

Data refinement extends operation refinement by allowing the state space of the concrete operations to be different from the state space of the abstract operations. It allows the mathematical data types of a specification to be replaced by more computer-oriented data types in a design.

A step of data refinement relates an *abstract* data type, the specification, to a *concrete* data type, the design. In fact, the concrete data type is another abstract data type, in the sense that it consists of a state space and some operations described by schemas. In this section, we shall call the state space of the abstract data type *Astate*, and the state space of the concrete data type *Cstate*. These state space schemas must not have any components in common. We shall use the names *Aop* and *Cop* to refer to an operation on the abstract state space, and the corresponding operation which implements it on the concrete data space. These operations have input $x? : X$ and output $y! : Y$.

In order to prove that the concrete data type correctly implements the abstract data type, we must explain which concrete states represent which abstract states. This is done with an *abstraction schema*, which we shall call *Abs*. This schema relates abstract and concrete states: it has the same signature as *Astate* $\wedge$ *Cstate*, and its property holds if the concrete state is one of those which represent the abstract state. It is quite usual for one abstract state to be represented by many concrete states. As an example, finite sets can be represented by sequences in which the order of elements does not matter; in this representation, a set of size n can be represented by any one of n factorial different sequences with the elements in different orders.

It is also possible for several abstract states to be represented by the same concrete state; this can happen if the abstract state contains information which cannot be extracted by any of the operations on the abstract data type. However, a simpler set of rules applies to the case where each concrete state represents a unique abstract state: this simpler set is listed in the last part of this section. It is not necessary for every abstract state to be represented, but only enough of them that one possible result of each execution of an operation on the type is represented. This means that abstract states which can never be reached using the operations need not be represented.

There are two conditions which must be satisfied for a data refinement to be correct, and they are analogues of the two conditions of operation refinement. The first condition ensures that the concrete operation terminates whenever the abstract operation is guaranteed to terminate. If an abstract state and a concrete state are related by the abstraction schema *Abs*, and the abstract state satisfies the pre-condition of the abstract operation, then the concrete state must satisfy the pre-condition of the concrete operation. In symbols:

$$\forall Astate;\ Cstate;\ x?:X \bullet$$
$$\text{pre } Aop \land Abs \Rightarrow \text{pre } Cop$$

The second condition ensures that the state after the concrete operation represents one of those abstract states in which the abstract operation could terminate. If an abstract state and a concrete state are related by *Abs*, and both the abstract and concrete operations are guaranteed to terminate, then every possible state after the concrete operation must be related by *Abs'* to a possible state after the abstract operation. In symbols:

$$\forall Astate;\ Cstate;\ Cstate';\ x?:X;\ y!:Y \bullet$$
$$\text{pre } Aop \land Abs \land Cop \Rightarrow (\exists Astate' \bullet Abs' \land Aop)$$

These two conditions should be proved for each operation on the data types.

A third condition relates the initial states of the abstract and concrete types. Each possible initial state of the concrete type must represent a possible initial state of the abstract type. In symbols:

$$\forall Cstate \bullet Cinit \Rightarrow$$
$$(\exists Astate \bullet Ainit \land Abs)$$

5.7 Functional refinement

A simpler set of conditions can be used if the abstraction schema, when viewed as a relation between concrete states and abstract states, is a total function. This property of *Abs* is expressed by the predicate

$$\forall Cstate \bullet \exists_1 Astate \bullet Abs$$

The first condition is the same as before:

$$\forall Astate;\ Cstate;\ x?:X \bullet$$
$$\text{pre } Aop \land Abs \Rightarrow \text{pre } Cop$$

The existential quantifier in the second condition can be avoided: the second condition simplifies to

$\forall\, Astate;\ Astate';\ Cstate;\ Cstate';\ x?:X;\ y!:Y\ \bullet$
$\quad \text{pre } Aop \wedge Abs \wedge Cop \wedge Abs' \Rightarrow Aop$

The third condition can also be simplified to avoid the existential quantifier:

$\forall\, Astate;\ Cstate \bullet Cinit \wedge Abs \Rightarrow Ainit$

These simplified conditions are equivalent to the general ones if the abstraction schema is a total function. Their advantage is that the proof that *Abs* is functional need be done only once for the whole data type, and this work does not have to be repeated for each operation.

CHAPTER SIX

Syntax Summary

This syntax summary supplements the syntax rules in Chapter 3 by making precise the binding powers of various constructs and collecting all the rules in one place.

The same conventions about repeated and optional phrases are used here as in Chapter 3; S, ..., S stands for a list of one or more instances of the class S separated by commas, and S; ...; S stands for one or more instances of S separated by semicolons. The notation S ... S stands for one or more adjacent instances of S with no separators. Phrases enclosed in slanted square brackets are optional.

The possibility of eliding semicolons which separate items both above and below the line in the three kinds of boxes has been made explicit here; these items are separated by instances of the class Sep, which may be either semicolons or newlines (NL). The rule given in Section 3.1.3 which allows extra newlines to be inserted before or after certain symbols is not made explicit in the grammar, however.

Certain collections of symbols have a range of binding powers: they are the logical connectives, used in predicates and schema expressions, the special-purpose schema operators, and infix function symbols, used in expressions. The relative binding powers of the logical connectives are indicated by listing them in decreasing order of binding power; the binding powers of infix function symbols are given in Section 3.1.2. Each production for which a binding power is relevant has been marked with an upper-case letter at the right margin; 'L' marks a symbol which associates to the left – so $A \wedge B \wedge C$ means $(A \wedge B) \wedge C$ – and 'R' marks a symbol which associates to the right. Unary symbols are marked with 'U'.

Specification   ::=   Paragraph NL ... NL Paragraph

Paragraph   ::=   [Ident, ..., Ident]
    | Axiomatic-Box
    | Schema-Box
    | Generic-Box
    | Schema-Name $\lceil$Gen-Formals$\rfloor$ $\hat{=}$ Schema-Exp
    | Def-Lhs == Expression
    | Ident ::= Branch | ... | Branch
    | Predicate

Axiomatic-Box   ::= $\lceil$
    | Decl-Part
    |———————
    | Axiom-Part $\rfloor$

Schema-Box   ::= $\lceil$
    —Schema-Name $\lceil$Gen-Formals$\rfloor$——
    | Decl-Part
    |————————
    | Axiom-Part $\rfloor$

Generic-Box   ::= $\lceil$
    —$\lceil$Gen-Formals$\rfloor$————————
    | Decl-Part
    |————————
    | Axiom-Part $\rfloor$

Decl-Part   ::=   Basic-Decl Sep ... Sep Basic-Decl

Axiom-Part   ::=   Predicate Sep ... Sep Predicate

Sep   ::=   ; | NL

Def-Lhs   ::=   Var-Name $\lceil$Gen-Formals$\rfloor$
    | Pre-Gen Ident
    | Ident In-Gen Ident

Branch   ::=   Ident
    | Var-Name $\langle\!\langle$Expression$\rangle\!\rangle$

Schema-Exp   ::= $\forall$ Schema-Text $\bullet$ Schema-Exp
    | $\exists$ Schema-Text $\bullet$ Schema-Exp
    | $\exists_1$ Schema-Text $\bullet$ Schema-Exp
    | Schema-Exp-1

Schema-Exp-1	::=	[Schema-Text]	
	|	Schema-Ref	
	|	¬ Schema-Exp-1	U
	|	pre Schema-Exp-1	U
	|	Schema-Exp-1 ∧ Schema-Exp-1	L
	|	Schema-Exp-1 ∨ Schema-Exp-1	L
	|	Schema-Exp-1 ⇒ Schema-Exp-1	R
	|	Schema-Exp-1 ⇔ Schema-Exp-1	L
	|	Schema-Exp-1 ⌈ Schema-Exp-1	L
	|	Schema-Exp-1 \ (Decl-Name, ... , Decl-Name)	L
	|	Schema-Exp-1 ⨟ Schema-Exp-1	L
	|	(Schema-Exp)	
Schema-Text	::=	Declaration *[| Predicate]*	
Schema-Ref	::=	Schema-Name Decoration *[Gen-Actuals]*	
Declaration	::=	Basic-Decl; ... ; Basic-Decl	
Basic-Decl	::=	Decl-Name, ... , Decl-Name : Expression	
	|	Schema-Ref	
Predicate	::=	∀ Schema-Text • Predicate	
	|	∃ Schema-Text • Predicate	
	|	$\exists_1$ Schema-Text • Predicate	
	|	Predicate-1	
Predicate-1	::=	Expression Rel Expression Rel ... Rel Expression	
	|	Pre-Rel Expression	
	|	Schema-Ref	
	|	pre Schema-Ref	
	|	*true*	
	|	*false*	
	|	¬ Predicate-1	U
	|	Predicate-1 ∧ Predicate-1	L
	|	Predicate-1 ∨ Predicate-1	L
	|	Predicate-1 ⇒ Predicate-1	R
	|	Predicate-1 ⇔ Predicate-1	L
	|	(Predicate)	
Rel	::=	= | ∈ | In-Rel	
Expression-0	::=	λ Schema-Text • Expression	
	|	μ Schema-Text *[• Expression]*	
	|	Expression	

Expression	::=	Expression In-Gen Expression	R
	|	Expression-1 $\times$ Expression-1 $\times \ldots \times$ Expression-1	
	|	Expression-1	
Expression-1	::=	Expression-1 In-Fun Expression-1	L
	|	$\mathbb{P}$ Expression-3	
	|	Pre-Gen Expression-3	
	|	$-$ Expression-3	
	|	Expression-3 Post-Fun	
	|	Expression-3^{Expression}	
	|	Expression-3 $($ Expression-0 $)$	
	|	Expression-2	
Expression-2	::=	Expression-2 Expression-3	
	|	Expression-3	
Expression-3	::=	Var-Name $\lceil$Gen-Actuals$\rfloor$	
	|	Number	
	|	Schema-Ref	
	|	Set-Expression	
	|	$\langle$ $\lceil$Expression, $\ldots$, Expression$\rfloor$ $\rangle$	
	|	$[\![$ $\lceil$Expression, $\ldots$, Expression$\rfloor$ $]\!]$	
	|	(Expression, $\ldots$, Expression)	
	|	θ Schema-Name Decoration	
	|	Expression-3 . Var-Name	
	|	(Expression-0)	

Note: The syntax of set expressions (Set-Exp) is ambiguous: if S is a schema, the expression $\{\, S \,\}$ may be either a (singleton) set display or a set comprehension, equivalent to $\{\, S \bullet \theta S \,\}$. The expression should be interpreted as a set comprehension; the set display can be written $\{(S)\}$.

Set-Exp	::=	$\{\, \lceil$Expression, $\ldots$, Expression$\rfloor \,\}$
	|	$\{\,$ Schema-Text $\lceil \bullet$ Expression$\rfloor \,\}$
Ident	::=	Word Decoration
Decl-Name	::=	Ident | Op-Name
Var-Name	::=	Ident | (Op-Name)
Op-Name	::=	$\_$ In-Sym $\_$ | Pre-Sym $\_$ | $\_$ Post-Sym | $\_$ $($ $\_$ $)$ | $-$
In-Sym	::=	In-Fun | In-Gen | In-Rel
Pre-Sym	::=	Pre-Gen | Pre-Rel

Post-Sym	::=	Post-Fun
Decoration	::=	⌈Stroke ... Stroke⌋
Gen-Formals	::=	[Ident, ... , Ident]
Gen-Actuals	::=	[Expression, ... , Expression]

Here is a list of the classes of terminal symbols used in the grammar:

Word	Undecorated name or special symbol
Stroke	Single decoration: ', ?, ! or a subscript digit
Schema-Name	Same as Word, but used to name a schema
In-Fun	Infix function symbol
In-Rel	Infix relation symbol
In-Gen	Infix generic symbol
Pre-Rel	Prefix relation symbol
Pre-Gen	Prefix generic symbol
Post-Fun	Postfix function symbol
Number	Unsigned decimal integer

The brilliant, articulate, white-eyelashed Mr. Zed turns his eyes to his wife and sees nothing but $Tx^{1}/_4\,p^{3}/_4 = {}^{1}/_2 - prx^{1}/_4$ (inverted).

Mervyn Peake, *Titus Alone*

Glossary

abstraction schema In data refinement, a schema which documents the relationship between the abstract and concrete state spaces. (p. 139)

basic type A named type denoting a set of objects regarded as atomic in a specification. (p. 27)

binding An object with one or more components named by identifiers. Bindings are the elements of *schema types*. (p. 28)

Cartesian product type A type $t_1 \times t_2 \times \cdots \times t_n$ containing ordered n-tuples $(x_1, x_2, \ldots, x_n)$ of objects drawn from n other types. (p. 27)

constraint A declaration may require that the values of the variables it introduces should satisfy a certain property. This property is the constraint of the declaration. (p. 31)

data refinement The process of showing that one set of operations is implemented by another set operating on a different state space. Data refinement allows the mathematical data types of a specification to be replaced in a design by more computer-oriented data types. (p. 137)

derived component A component of a schema describing the state space of an abstract data type whose value can be deduced from the values of the other components. (p. 4)

extension One *situation* is an extension of another if and only if the second situation is a *restriction* of the first to a smaller signature. (p. 33)

finitary construction A construction which may consistently be used on the right-hand side of a free type definition. Many constructions which involve only finite objects are finitary. (p. 84)

graph The set of ordered pairs of objects for which a binary relation holds. In Z, relations are modelled by their graphs. (p. 29)

implicit pre-condition A pre-condition of an operation which is not explicitly stated in its specification, but is implicitly part of the post-condition or of the invariant on the final state. (p. 132)

join Two *type-compatible* signatures can be joined to form a signature that has all the variables of both the original ones, with the same types. (p. 33)

logically equivalent Two predicates are logically equivalent if they express the same property, that is, if they are true in exactly the same situations. (p. 31)

loose specification A specification in which the values of the global variables are not completely determined by the predicates which constrain them. (p. 135)

non-deterministic An operation in an *abstract data type* is non-deterministic if there may be more than one possible state after execution of the operation for a single state before it. (p. 133)

operation refinement The process of showing that one operation is implemented by another with the same state space. In its general form, this allows constructs from a programming language to be introduced into a design. (p. 137)

pre-condition The condition on the state before an operation and on its inputs that there should exist a possible state afterwards and outputs satisfying its post-condition. (p. 132)

predicate A formula describing a relationship between the values of the variables in a *signature*. (p. 30)

property The mathematical relationship expressed by a predicate. A property is characterized by the *situations* in which it is true. (p. 31)

restriction The restriction of a *situation* for one *signature* to another signature is defined if the second signature is a sub-signature of the first. Each variable is given the same value by the restriction as by the original situation, and variables not in the smaller signature are ignored. (p. 33)

schema A *signature* together with a *property* relating the variables of the signature. (p. 31)

schema type A type $\langle p_1 : t_1;\ p_2 : t_2;\ \ldots;\ p_n : t_n \rangle$ containing *bindings* with components named $p_1, p_2, \ldots, p_n$ drawn from other types. (p. 28)

scope rules A set of rules which determine what identifiers may be used at each point in a specification and what definition each of them refers to. (p. 36)

sequential composition The sequential composition $Op1 \,\fatsemi\, Op2$ of two operation schemas $Op1$ and $Op2$ describes a composite operation in which first $Op1$ then $Op2$ occurs. (p. 136)

set type A type $\mathbb{P}\ t$ containing the sets of objects drawn from another type t. (p. 27)

signature A collection of variables, each with a type. (p. 30)

situation A situation determines the values of the variables in a signature. For each signature, there are many situations, each giving the variables different values drawn from their types. (p. 30)

state space The set of *states* which an abstract data type can have. In Z, the state space is specified by a schema with the same name as the abstract data type. None of the components of this schema should have a decoration. (p. 130)

sub-signature One signature is a sub-signature of another one if the second contains all the variables of the first, with the same types. (p. 33)

type The type of an expression determines a set in which the value of the expression lies. There are four kinds of types: *basic types*, *set types*, *Cartesian product types*, and *schema types*. (p. 26)

type compatible Two signatures are type compatible if each variable common to both signatures has the same type in each of them. Many of the operations on schemas demand that their arguments have type compatible signatures. (p. 33)

Index of symbols

General index

Entries set in *italic* type are the names of constants in the mathematical tool-kit. Special symbols are indexed here under a descriptive name; the symbol itself is shown in parentheses. The one-page 'Index of symbols' lists all these symbols for ease of reference. Entries set in sans-serif type are syntactic categories; they refer to the pages where the syntax rules for the categories may be found.